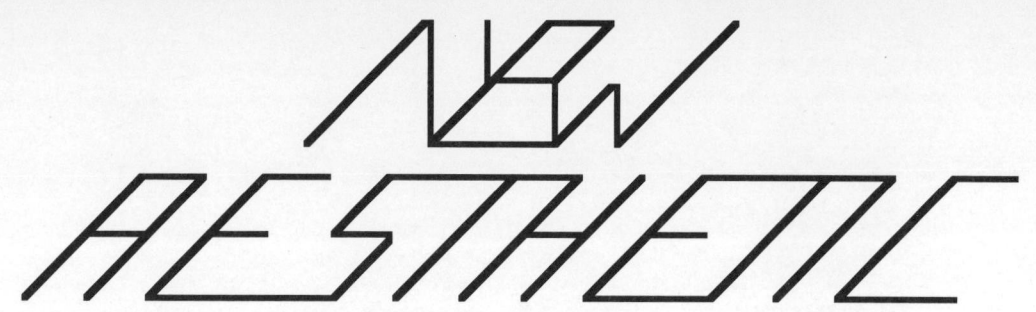

New Aesthetic 1

A Collection of Experimental and Independent Type Design

Edited by Leonhard Laupichler & Sophia Brinkgerd

Sorry Press®

Typography is the heartbeat of graphic design. It's more than the gateway to an enjoyable and efficient reading experience. It's a language that expresses more than mere words and sentences—an art form that speaks volumes in silence.

New Aesthetic delves into the enigmatic realms of creative expression, uniting a collective of typographers, artists, and designers, each contributing their distinctive approach to typography. New Aesthetic seeks to inspire and innovate, opposing typographic rigidity and welcoming artistic exploration and expressive experimentation.

New Aesthetic believes in the profound emotional influence wielded by typefaces and serves as a canvas, painting a multifaceted portrait of modern typography. Focusing on this potential for deep impact that typefaces possess, New Aesthetic shows modern typography in a multitude of facets. In this revised and reworked edition of the very first unpublished volume of New Aesthetic, we are continuing the journey through independent type design.

The Editors

12:15
Colin Doerffler

The 12:51 font was created in 2016 as part of the installation piece "My Voice Found the Words I Sought," which visualizes the interplay between words, images, and reality,—how they define, mask and manipulate each other. 12:51 first emerged as an expression of studies concerning the simultaneous evolution of phonographic and ideographic font developments, as well as an interpretation of current tendencies of the recursive imagery of alphabetic writings.

12:51 is a hybrid font that integrates elements from both Latin and Chinese alphabets. The letter structures are modular and draw inspiration from the contrasts between calligraphic and digital design elements. Overall, 12:51 is a provocation to our reading habits and the way we perceive forms, ultimately highlighting the space that exists between words and images.

Classification
Display
Monospace

Styles
N/A

Release
Display 2018, Mono 2019

Contact
colindoerffler.com
@colindoerffler

Aegi
Christian Horrer, Mario Naegele

The Aegi typeface is the result of a joint student project by Christian Horrer and Mario Naegele, whose goal was to get closer to the basic processes of type design and to gain initial experience. Therefore, the design of the typeface is primarily based on several tests with pen and ink, drawings, and experiments with lead type. Inspired by birds' beaks, the typeface is characterized by a slightly unpredictable behavior, strong contrasts, and sharp edges.

Classification
Serif

Styles
Regular

Release
2021

Contact
christian-horrer.com
@errhor201
marionaegele.de
@mario.nae

Aegi Serif ©
→Regular
Typeface —
* 2021
© Aegi Serif
Regular ←
— Typeface
2021 *

AEGI SERIF
REGULAR
TYPEFACE

CHRISTIAN HORRER
MARIO NAEGELE

Airdancer
Massimiliano Audretsch, Moritz Appich, Bruno Jacoby (Gruppo Due)

In the dimly lit sanctum of typographic innovation, Gruppo Due witnessed the birth of Airdancer as a non-revivalist whisper against conformity. From the timeworn roots of linear antiqua typefaces, this enigmatic typeface emerged with a shy dance, a cadence known only to those who observed its mysterious evolution.

Defying tradition, Airdancer moves gracefully between slender grace and voluptuous curves as a variable, two-axis typeface. It embodies a mercurial spirit, much like the elusive character of its wiggly counterpart outside the world of typography. Look at it glowing as it waves its arms in a sunlit suburban garden. Airdancer proudly displays the freshly designed typeface on its tubular body. Dancing with the wind. Smiling.

Classification
Sans Serif

Styles
Variable on two axes
with 21+ Styles

Release
2024

Contact
gruppo-due.com
@gruppo.due

ALBINO
Lukas Manuel Altmann

ALBINO is a hybrid typeface—a reinterpretation of classic Fraktur elements paired with the dynamism of script typefaces and deliberate grotesque influences. The creation of ALBINO was based on a very traditional approach. Working with a nib pen, ink, and tracing paper allowed me to develop a wide variety of individual letters in a short period of time without getting lost in the details. During this process, I came across a close-up of an albino alligator by French photographer Emma Panchot. This image was a great source of inspiration. For me, it embodies the essence of the characteristics of ALBINO. It is strange, almost mystical. A calm and majestic lurking animal, surrounded by a violent aura. Dynamic, radical and yet so elegant. Bringing these apparent contradictions into a harmonious balance is the foundation of the typeface.

Classification
Hybrid

Styles
Regular

Release
N/A

Contact
lmaltmann.com
@lmaltmann

DNA
ALBINO

DNA
ALBINO

DNA
ALBINO

TYR

OCA2

APK Galeria
Peter Korsman (Autograph)

APK Galeria is a modern grotesque typeface family firmly rooted in the modernist aesthetic. The characteristic combination of well-known grotesque features with harder cuts and subtleties are the details that make the typeface visually distinctive and instantly recognizable, while maintaining its versatility. Galeria was designed with the intention of taking the characteristics (neutral, rational) of the modern grotesque to the extreme. Without losing sight of the essentials of usability and legibility. APK Galeria is a real workhorse. A typeface with a palpable gravity that has the uniqueness to be used in logotypes and the versatility to be used as a display face. APK Galeria is available in seven weights with accompanying Italics. It offers large character sets and four style sets of alternates across the weights. It was originally designed in 2016 as a custom font (Regular) as part of a visual identity for a modern art gallery in the Netherlands. Now, in 2022, it has been revisited, reworked, and refined. Together with Swiss-based type designer Maël Bächtold, the Regular has been expanded into a complete typeface family and released in 2023 with the launch of APK Type.

Classification
Modern Grotesk

Styles

Thin	**Bold**
Light	**Extrabold**
Regular	**Italics**
Medium	
Semibold	

Release
2023

Contact
apk-type.com
@autograph__

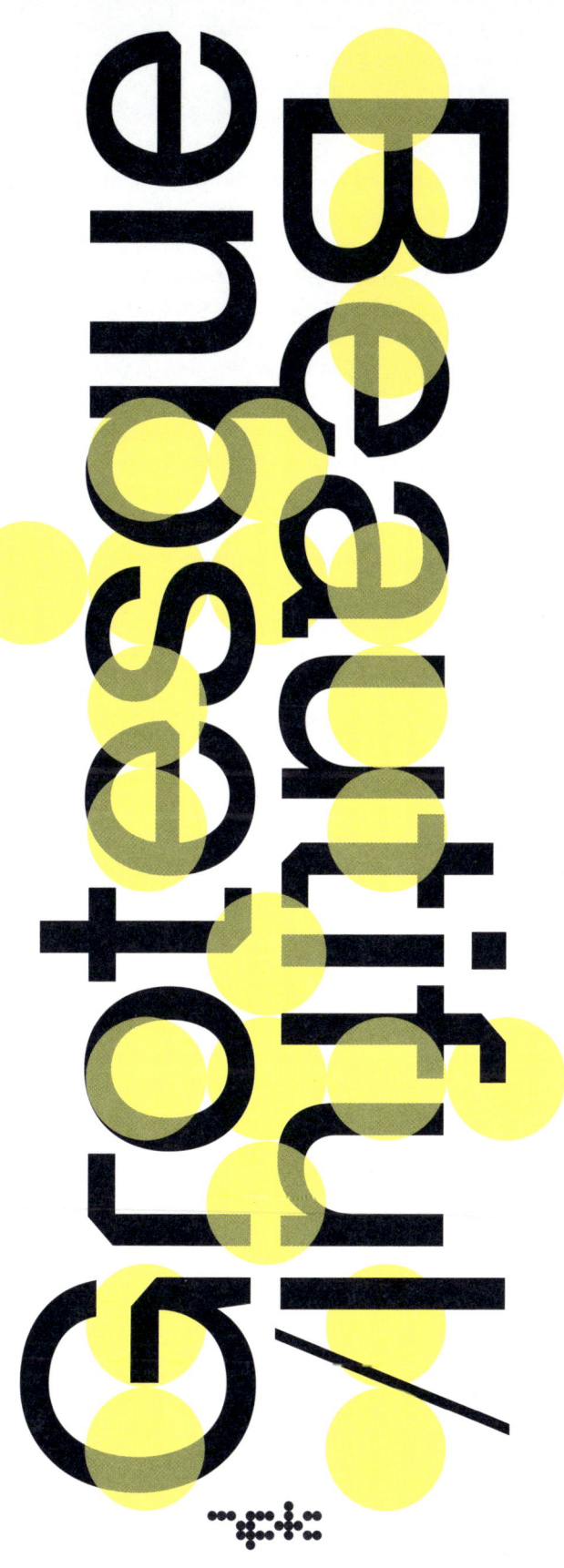

Apparat
Michael Clasen, Marcel Saidov (kimera)

Apparat is inspired by early 70's typefaces optimized for television. The counters have much stronger curves than the outer forms, and the junctions are opened up by large ink traps. This gives it its distinctive mechanical look and creates a very high legibility on screen and paper. It caricatures traditional letterforms, making the design language extremely concise. Apparat is a versatile workhorse, designed for use in both display and text sizes. It comes with several features like digital time alternates, clock symbols for each hour, and many more.

Classification
Grotesk

Styles
Light	**Heavy**
Regular	**Black**
Book	
Medium	
Bold	

Release
2023

Contact
kimeracorp.eu
@kimeracorp

01:23 → 01 23

06:41 → 06 41

QUANTUM LEAPS

OMEGA
Union Glashütte
HAF 912+

Munich
05 25 05 40
Istanbul
08 30 08 50

Quartz
Tourbillon
Dial
CALIBER
Bezel
Pallet Fork
Crown
Slide Rule

AM
UTC
PM

Arachne
Leonhard Laupichler

As I worked on the Arachne typeface, I reinterpreted common elements found in classical typefaces, which is why I chose to call it a new classicist typeface. Arachne's strength stems from the seamless fusion of soft strokes and sharp, edgy details that instantly catch the eye. The dynamic curves and carefully designed axis infuse Arachne with a soft yet vibrant character, combining contrasting elements of classicist and modern styles, thick and thin strokes, and dynamic yet structured shapes.

Developing Arachne involved a lot of experimentation. I sought to incorporate innovative, distinctive, and attention-grabbing elements to create a unique typeface without going overboard. After completing the regular version, I went on to create two more playful variants named "Demigod" and "Divine," gently exaggerating Arachne's special features. Then, in April 2020, I introduced the extraordinary "Demonic" style, maximizing the impact of the serifs for a truly remarkable expression.

Classification
New Classicist

Styles
Mortal
Demigod
Divine
Demonic

Release
2019

Contact
leonhardlaupichler.com
@leonhardlaupichler

ARACHNE/ MORTAL AND DIVINE/

NEW CLASSICIST AVAILABLE IN EARLY JUNE 2019 INSPIRED BY A GREEK MYTH

Savage, Venomous, Pleasant, Edgy, Graceful, Attractive!

MOST DANGEROUS SPIDERS ON EARTH

1.	Phoneutria nigriventer	6.	Missulena tussulena
2.	Atrax robustus	7.	Poecilotheria ornata
3.	Loxosceles reclusa	8.	Cheiracanthium
4.	Latrodectus hesperus	9.	Solifugae
5.	Hexophthalma hahni	10.	Tegenaria agrestis

ARACHNE Demofont 2020   TYPEDESIGN Leonhard Laupichler

Architype 45 / 90
Sascha Bente

Architype 45 / 90 is a stencil typeface developed in a workshop
with NORM as part of the Type Design Masters program at ECAL.
It emerged from the visual heritage of De Stijl Architypes by Theo
van Doesburg and Bart Van Der Leck. Following a strict system, all
straight lines are forced to follow a 90 and 45 degree angle, as
Doesburg created a right angle alphabet and Van Der Leck opened
up this approach to include 45 degrees. The stencil itself consists
of 12 differently sized bars that must be arranged on a surface to form
letters freely.

Classification
Experimental Stencil

Styles
Regular 45
Regular 90

Release
2019

Contact
saschabente.com
@sascha.bente

THERE IS AN OLD AND A NEW CON-CIOUS-NESS OF TIME.

SET IN ARCHITYPE 45/90 BY SASCHA BENTE

E OLD IS CONNECTED WITH
E INDIVIDUAL.

E NEW IS CONNECTED WITH
E UNIVERSAL.

ANIFESTO 1 OF DE STIJL,
RTICLE 3, NOVEMBER 1918

Atlanta
Basile Fournier

I wanted to create a typeface that focused more on the individual forms of the letters, as if each letter could be an illustration or a graphic element, so that each letter offered specific details and an original form. I experimented with the ink trap options of the RoboFont software and played around with the different variations of this tool. I wanted to create a playful yet beautiful typeface, but it's more of a display typeface and works well for headlines or posters.

 I listen to a lot of US rap from Atlanta, where the whole trap movement started. I thought it would be interesting to associate this typeface and use it to reference lyrics by my favorite Atlanta rappers, and also to write the addresses of the trap houses where the music originally came from. I also thought it was funny to play with the word "trap" from the ink traps and link it to this trap music scene in Atlanta.

Classification
Serif

Styles
Regular

Release
2019

Contact
@basilefournier

'2023'
[AT]-GA
Piedmont
Park 14.

The term "trap" is commonly used to designate the locale where illicit drug transactions take place. Its origins trace back to Atlanta, Georgia, where renowned rappers like Cool Breeze, Dungeon Family, Outkast, Goodie Mob, and Ghetto Mafia were among the pioneers incorporating this term into their musical expressions. In 1988, one of the earliest recorded instances was found in UGK's "Cocaine In The Back of the Ride" from their debut EP, "The Southern Way." Fast forward to 1992, they followed up with the widely recognized "Pocket Full of Stones" as part of their major-label debut album, "Too Hard to Swallow." This track even found its way into the 1993 film "Menace II Society."

Atlanta Typeface by Basile Fournier©

2020—2023

The term "trap" is commonly used to designate the locale where illicit drug transactions take place. Its origins trace back to Atlanta, Georgia, where renowned rappers like Cool Breeze, Dungeon Family, Outkast, Goodie Mob, and Ghetto Mafia were among the pioneers incorporating this term into their musical expressions. In 1988, one of the earliest recorded instances was found in UGK's "Cocaine In The Back of the Ride" from their debut EP, "The Southern Way." Fast forward to 1992, they followed up with the widely recognized "Pocket Full of Stones" as part of their major-label debut album, "Too Hard to Swallow." This track even found its way into the 1993 film "Menace II Society."

'Atl=

AURAE
Janik Sandbothe

AURAE dares to combine the two rival worlds of functionalism and extravagance in a Sans Serif typeface. AURAE has four stylistic weights. The first extreme point is a cut with the greatest possible straightness and simplicity. Two intermediate steps lead to the other extreme, which is characterized by contrasting strokes and extravagant curves. By creating AURAE as a variable typeface, users can decide exactly how much functionalism and how much flamboyance they want in their Sans Serif. The character of an end product can be perfectly supported by a custom font. AURAE is inspired by the characteristics of the wind. It contains a motionless stillness, a slight movement, as well as the unpredictable eruption of stormy gusts.

Classification
Sans Serif

Styles
Calm
Breeze
Gale
Storm

Release
N/A

Contact
janiksandbothe.de
@janiksandbothe

WATCHING THE FLOW OF

It was one of those march days when the sun shines hot and the wind blows ~ cold: when it is summer in the light, and winter in the shade.

A CALMING BREEZE

Janik Sandbothe

Bad Mono
Tor Weibull

Bad Mono is a monospaced typeface inspired by badminton. It's influenced by the rhythm of the game and the net of the court, which is made up of a grid. When the shuttlecock hits the net, the grid squares of the net expand. Inspired by this, most of the uppercase letters are twice as wide as the lowercase letters, as if the ball had just hit them and expanded them. The monospaced nature of the typeface ensures that the letters align, creating structure in the rhythm. The typeface was originally created for photographer Carl Oliver Anders' exhibition "A Game of Badminton" in 2016.

Classification
Reversed Contrast

Styles
Monospace

Release
2016

Contact
kanonfoundry.com
@tweibull

Baptiste
Sophia Brinkgerd

Baptiste is the result of years of creative exploration and experimentation with classical typefaces, drawing inspiration from the grandeur of classical book art and storytelling, all embodied in the form of a modern Serif Display typeface. Its shapes reflect a creative process heavily influenced by antique book design and the timeless sense of proportion and elegance found in calligraphy. It aims to capture a sense of playfulness in its details while maintaining an element of grace.

Baptiste also seeks to visually encapsulate the essence of classical literature and its iconic heroes, echoing the romance and eloquence of words written with quill and ink. It does so with a modern approach to display typefaces, all while paying homage to the rich historical heritage of serif typefaces.

Referencing the storytelling aspect, the artwork was inspired by the Beauchamp-Feuillet notation system. This system manages to convey the connection between music, motion, and emotion, telling a story through letterforms that transcend mere reading, creating a narrative beyond the letters themselves.

Classification
Display

Styles
Regular

Release
2024

Contact
sophiabrinkgerd.com
@sophiabrinkgerd

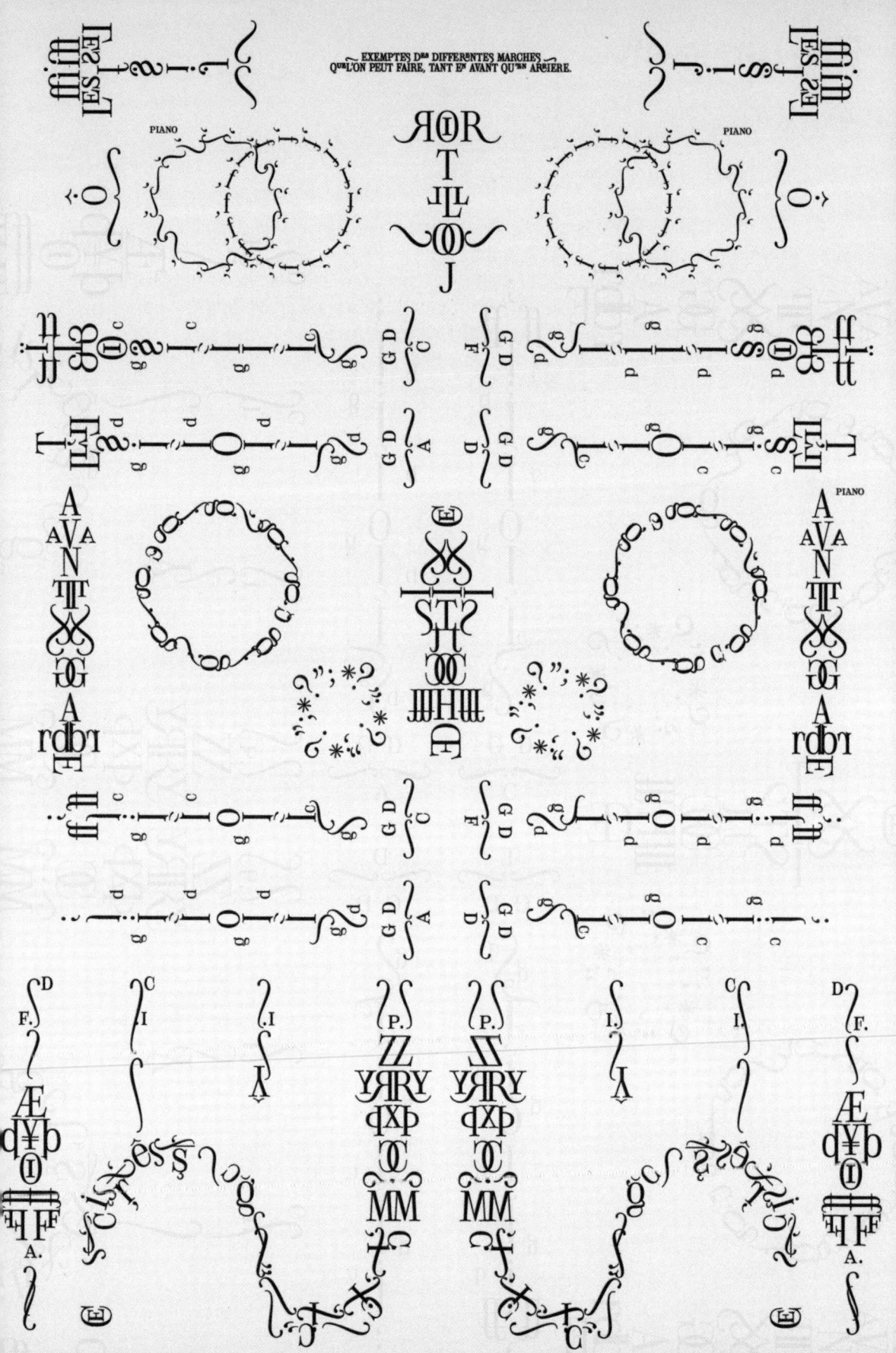

EXEMPTES DES DIFFERENTES MARCHES
QU'L'ON PEUT FAIRE, TANT EN AVANT QU'EN ARRIERE.

BedTimes.otf
Gunnar Harrison

BedTimes.otf is a self-initiated edit of Times New Roman and one of the first things I did with the Glyphs font design software. It didn't start with a concept or aesthetic in mind, which helped me not take it too seriously. I tinkered with anchor points and curves until I found interesting relationships with existing letterforms. At the time, I spontaneously decided on the name BedTimes.otf (I liked how it sounded), but I've since worked out a bit more of a concept: BedTimes.otf aims to communicate the subtle inconsistencies between our dreams and the lived experiences on which they're based by marrying foreign shapes with familiar letterforms.

Classification
Bootleg Serif

Styles
Regular

Release
2019

Contact
gunnaris.me
@gunnarisme

okayyy about to fall
asleep but here's
the character overview
for my bootleg font
BedTimes.otf
AaBbCcDdEeFfGg
HhIiJjKkLlMm
NnOoPpQqRrSsTtUu
VvWwXxYyZzZz
zzZzZzZzZzZzZzZz
ZzZzZzZz
ZzZzZzZz
Zz

Bigguy
Martin Pyšný

Bigguy was designed as a corporate typeface for a Slovak graphic studio in 2015. It was created to be used when working with photography and illustration, where it's used as a mask. The idea of visual communication of the studio was: Each project uses a capital letter as a mask of its mood image. This way each project has its own logo. It makes interesting patterns on web and social media. Bigguy is a monospace typeface with a square base. It is designed for large sizes and as a display type. It has two styles: Slim (outlined) and Fat (bold). Unfortunately, Bigguy was only used in the logo of this studio and has never been published.

Classification
Decorative

Styles
Fat
Slim

Release
N/A

Contact
matopysny.com
@mato.pysny

Bonnster
Neville Brody (Brody Associates)

In 1991, our studio was commissioned to create a new visual language and system for the Bundeskunsthalle in Bonn, Germany. Designed by Professor Gustav Peichl, it was an imposing postmodern building in denial of its heritage, and was based on core geometric shapes, which were then interrupted by wavy lines, curved arcs, circles, and cones. We created not only a system, but also a set of core components that would sit at the heart of the communications DNA, including a full set of contemporary icons and a new geometric-based typeface that we called Bonn.

Roll forwards thirty years, and we have been asked to revisit the brand language, modernising it and ensuring it would work successfully and scale across different platforms including digital and rich media. To coincide with this relaunch, the gallery installed a major exhibition on postmodernism. It felt natural to then update Bonn to align with the theme—a joyful task that allowed us to be ultimately playful and irreverent with the shapes of the letterforms, enabling it to be used in conjunction with the Bonn font.

Classification
Display

Styles
Ultra
Bold
Black

Release
N/A

Contact
brody-associates.com
@brody_associates

C-Raf
Baptiste Bernazeau

The development of the C-Raf family began in 2018 with a very traditional approach. I had to create a good part of the alphabet with a nip pen, and then adapt and refine the letters with tracing paper and ink. The whole approach was to find a compromise between a really fine typeface, while keeping a strong look and an ethereal feel. I decided to keep the rounded serifs as a reminder of the drawing process. During the whole making, I had images of flamingos and vultures in mind as a way to find a good middle ground between a tall size, a steady stance, and a great scope.

Classification
Garalde / Old Style

Styles
Light (C-Raf.1)
Regular (C-Raf.2)

Release
2019

Contact
@forge.cestainsi.online

C-Raf.1

PICASSO'S ANGELS
CrimsonSwan

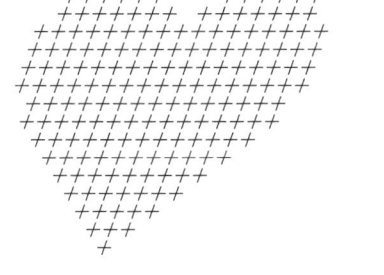

DivineStorm AltoJustizia AbsoluteTerror HuntingSeason SirenFlashes UniqueFlower MyriadPetals InfiniteFolds FuryFromTheSky RoadToApocalypse DreamFastBeforeYouPerish

AÆBCDEFGHIJKLM
NOŒPQRSTUVWXYZ
aæbcdefghijklm
noœpqrstuvwxyz
0123456789
["*"]/–––—&(?!«.,;.»)

Living Artifacts
In The Core Of The Volcano
FORGE is a type and sound webfoundry
powered by CESTAINSI online

L'Amour
7ISi
C'estLaVie

Charon
Matthieu Visentin

Inspired by the finesse and shadow play of engraved tombstones in a labyrinthine cemetery in Buenos Aires, Charon is a sculptural and minimalist typeface that adds an elegant and ethereal dimension to large titles. Its sharp serifs and high contrast are reminiscent of an engraver's chisel and the shadows cast by finely beveled epitaphs. The process was one of long walks and documenting photographs taken in the alleys of the cemetery. Originally, the typeface was intended to be condensed like the Latin characters found there, in order to keep only two elements that make up Charon's identity: high and tense contrasts, and pointed serifs that give it its impalpable solidity and airy feeling.

Classification
Display Serif

Styles
Regular
Italic

Release
2017

Contact
@kommak

René Guénon

Introduction Générale à l'Étude des Doctrines Hindoues [1921] • Théosophisme, histoire d'une Pseudo-Religion [1921] • L'Erreur Spirite [1923] • Orient et Occident [1924] • L'Ésotérisme de Dante [1925] • L'Homme et son Devenir selon le Vedanta [1925] • Le Roi du Monde [1927] • La Crise du Monde Moderne [1927] • Saint Bernard [1929] • Autorité Spirituelle et Pouvoir Temporel [1929] • Le Symbolisme de la Croix [1931] • Les États Multiples de l'Être [1932] • Métaphysique Orientale [1939] • Le Règne de la Quantité et les Signes des Temps [1945] • Principes du Calcul Infinitésimal [1946] • Aperçus sur l'Initiation [1946] • La Grande Triade [1946]

ComicStrip
Paul Bergès

The ComicStrip typeface is directly inspired by the aesthetics of onomatopoeia and shapes from the world of comics and cartoons. Its
rounded shapes and modular appearance reveal the naive and comical
side of this display fantasy character. For the ComicStrip typeface,
the idea was to reduce the set of letters in an alphabet (including uppercase, punctuation, and various glyphs) to a single module (two
circles and a diagonal) and a simple and circular grid. The font takes
its name from Serge Gainsbourg's song "Comic Strip", released in
1967 (in the spirit of the 1960s pop culture movement), whose lyrics are
composed of onomatopoeia.

Classification
Display

Styles
Regular

Release
2019

Contact
@begia__

260 PT

J'LENS PETITE FILLE DANS MON COOL-C STEP
J'LENS FAIRE DES RULES, J'LENS FAIRE DES WUP!
DES CLIP! CRAP! DES BANG! DES WLOP! ET DES 2WP!
SHEBAM! POW! BLOP! WIZZ! (3 FOIS)

N'AIS PAS PEUR BÉBÉ AGRR PPE-TPX CHRACK!
J'SUIS CLOSH POUR TOI PROTEGER TCHLACK!
FERME LES YEUX CRACK! DÉGRAISSE-WOI, SPACK!
SHEBAM! POW! BLOP! WIZZ!

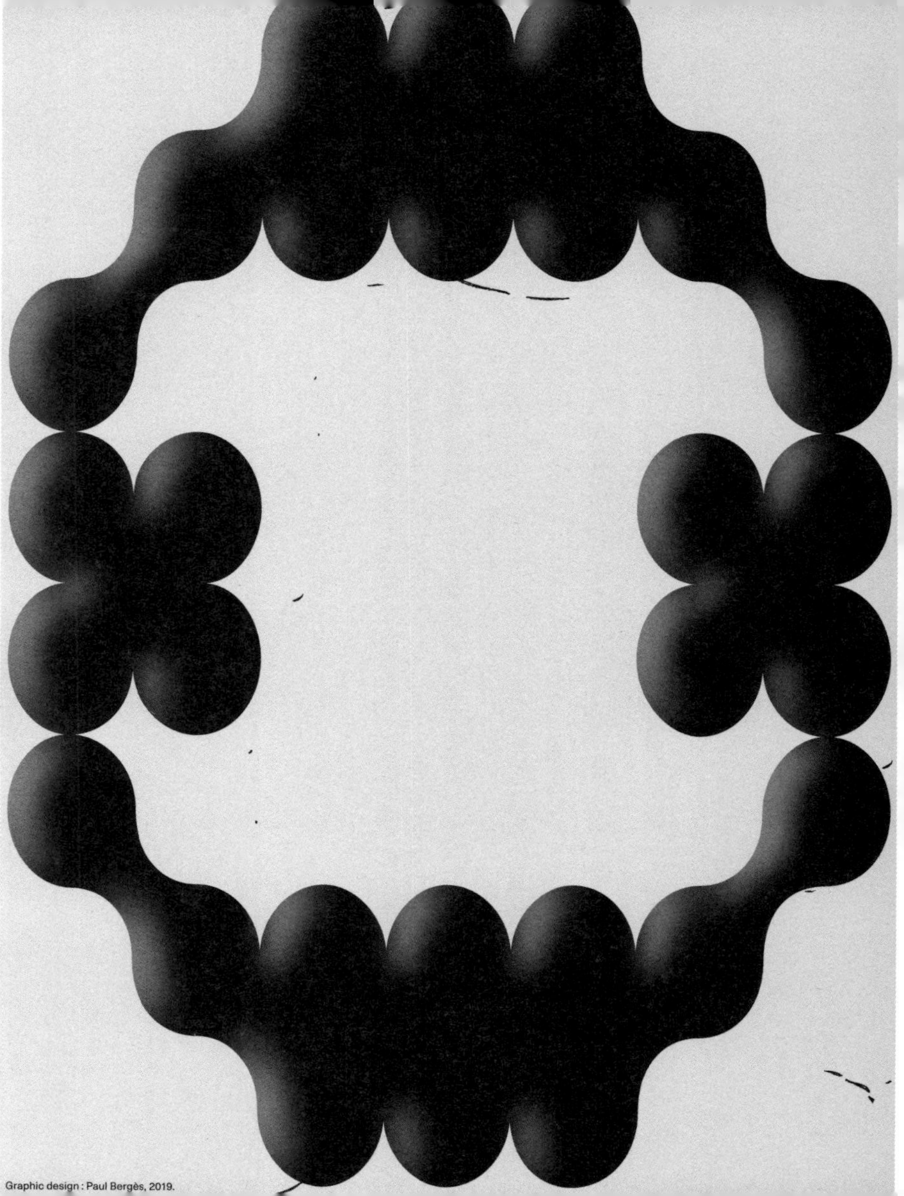

Cosmo
Mingoo Yoon

Cosmo is one of the projects of the Master's course at ECAL, a modern typeface family based on the lettering of the Palazzo dei Congressi. The building, located in the EUR district of Rome, Italy, was designed by Adalberto Libera and built between 1938 and 1954. The capitals were initially developed with small but delicate serifs within a high-contrast structure. The discrete ligatures are designed to match the atmosphere of the building and the history behind it. The typeface has been given a new geometric-modern style that explores the new field, which is different from the traditional Didone style.

Classification
Display
Serif

Styles
Regular

Release
N/A

Contact
yoonmingoo.net
@yoonmingoo

I AM A TOMBSTONE, AN IMAGE.
I AM A TOMBSTONE, AN IMAGE.
I AM A TOMBSTONE, AN IMAGE.
I AM A TOMBSTONE, AN IMAGE.
I AM A TOMBSTONE, AN IMAGE.
I AM A TOMBSTONE, AN IMAGE.
I AM A TOMBSTONE, AN IMAGE.
I AM A TOMBSTONE, AN IMAGE.
I AM A TOMBSTONE, AN IMAGE.
I AM A TOMBSTONE, AN IMAGE.
I AM A TOMBSTONE, AN IMAGE.
I AM A TOMBSTONE, AN IMAGE.
I AM A TOMBSTONE, AN IMAGE.
I AM A TOMBSTONE, AN IMAGE.
I AM A TOMBSTONE, AN IMAGE.
I AM A TOMBSTONE, AN IMAGE.

SEIKILOS PLACED ME HERE AS
A LONG-LASTING SIGN OF
DEATHLESS REMEMBRANCE.

WHILE YOU LIVE, SHINE
HAVE NO GRIEF AT ALL
LIFE EXISTS ONLY FOR A SHORT WHILE
AND TIME DEMANDS HIS DUE.

HÓSON ZÊIS, PHAÍNOU
MĒDÈN HÓLŌS SỲ LYPOÛ
PRÒS OLÍGON ÉSTI TÒ ZÊN
TÒ TÉLOS HO KHRÓNOS APAITEÎ.

Cryo
Pauline Le Pape

Cryo Display is a work-in-progress typeface that explores different sources of uncial typography and calligraphy, mostly found in Brittany (FR), where I come from. It aims to find a contemporary aesthetic for an outdated source.

Classification
Display

Styles
Regular

Release
N/A

Contact
@paulinelpape

Character overview 217

CyberSiberia
Timur Zima

This typeface is inspired by the monospaced typefaces synonymous with the Designers Republic studio. It can be seen in the fonts the studio created for the iconic Wipe Out video game series. Their work perfectly combines aesthetics and meaning.

     Beyond design homage, it encapsulates profound reflections on our future, especially in the Russian context. It blends artistic inspiration and socio-political commentary, embodying Brutalist plasticity through stark simplicity. The font's anti-utopian character subtly reflects Russia's tumultuous political landscape, reminding us of the constant struggle between artistic expression and oppression. In essence, it transcends typography, symbolizing human resilience in the face of adversity and illustrating the power of design to provoke thought and challenge dominant narratives.

Classification
Monospace Display

Styles
Regular

Release
2017

Contact
@timur_zima

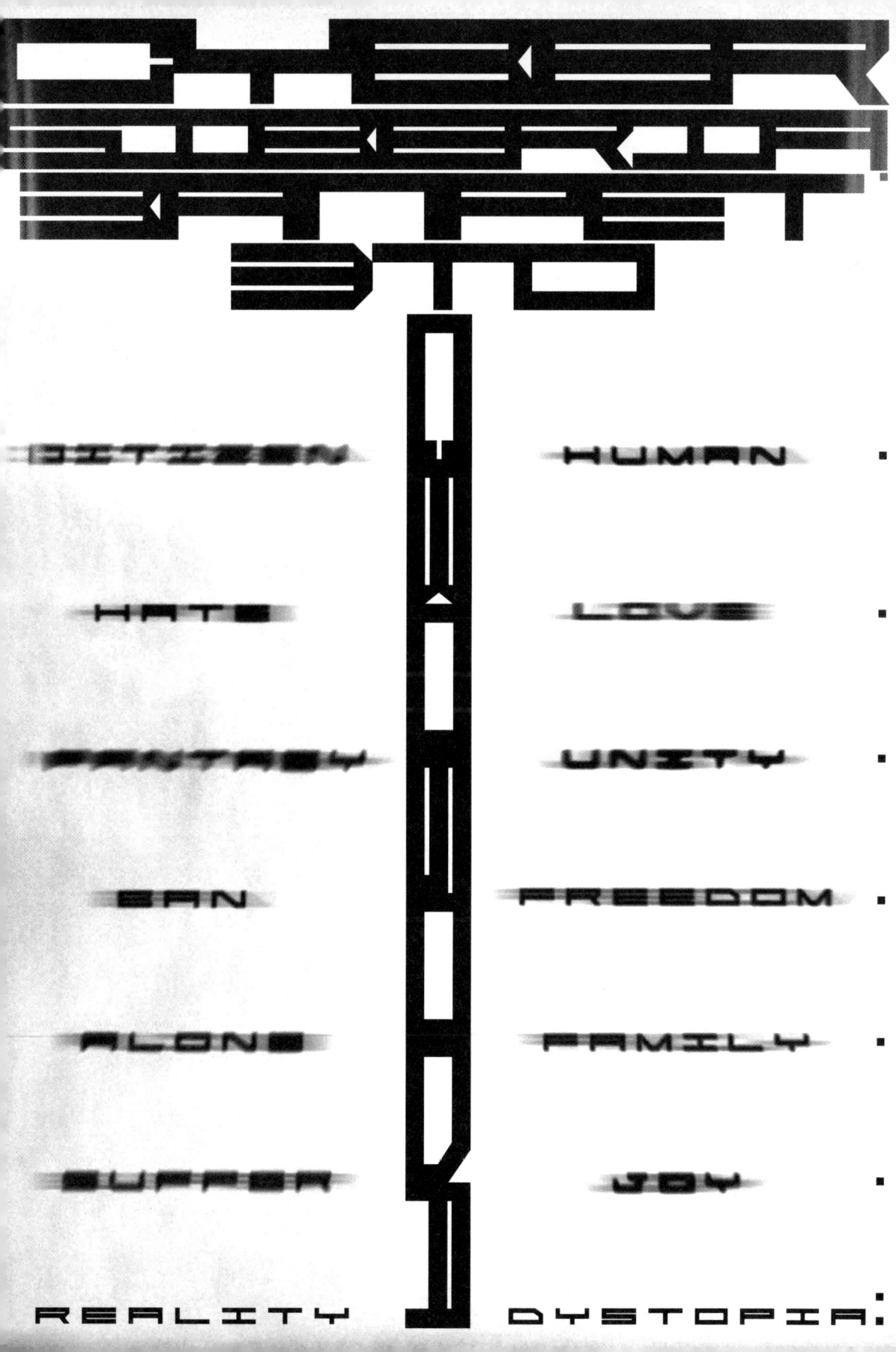

DaVinci
Virgile Flores

DaVinci is a fluid, display-friendly typeface with prominent serifs and a low x-height. Its forms are inspired by Garamond's work as an engraver of punches, the masters used to stamp matrices, the molds used to cast metal type. The point of this revival was to get as close as possible to the fluidity and organic shapes created by the ink as it is printed and expands on the paper. DaVinci is the second release of the Trojan Type Factory, a typographic foundry that combines elements and references from Greek mythology and malware. Its name is a reference to a software program for remote control of a Microsoft Windows computer system over a network.

Classification
Old Style Serif

Styles
Regular

Release
2019

Contact
virgileflores.com
@virgileflores

TRJN DaVinci

Trojan   Type   Factory

ABCD efgh
EFGH efgh
JKLMN ijklmn
OPQR opqr
STU V stuv
WXYZ wxyz
.,:;!?.•* 0123
456789
&

abcd

HACKING
KEYSTROKE
SOFTWARE
DATABASE
ELINT
REMOTE
ENCRIPTED
VERIZON
Hacking
Keystroke
Software
Database
Elint
Remote
Encripted
Verizon
HACKING
KEYSTROKE
SOFTWARE
DATABASE
ELINT
REMOTE
ENCRIPTED
VERIZON
Hacking
Keystroke
Software
Database
Elint
Remote
Encripted
Verizon

©®

Epingle
Victor Gérard (Various Glyphs)

Epingle was initiated in 2018, while studying in the typography department of La Cambre. It is a display typeface in which the letters are drawn in a single line, with bold areas when the directions change radically or when the line forms a junction. The first sketches of Epingle were drawn while listening to Jonny Trunk's Sister Woo, and the individual glyph designs give the impression of notes on a musical score. In 2022, overall metrics and design corrections were applied to improve the typeface and simplify font pairing. An Italic and Script style are in development, hopefully to be released by the end of 2024.

Classification
Calligraphic Decorative

Styles
Upright Display

Release
2019

Contact
victorgerard.fr
@gerardpointfr

EUPHORIA
Janik Sandbothe

Euphoria is a decorative and experimental display typeface with extreme stroke width contrasts and a single-stroke design. Its hairline-thin swirly strokes are accompanied by exaggerated ball terminals and qualify the typeface for an expressive use in larger font sizes. The inspiration for Euphoria can be found on the cover of the 40th Jugend issue from October 1897. Ludwig von Zumbusch illustrated the cover and letterforms that eventually became the foundation of my design. The Art Nouveau influence gives Euphoria its incomparable look and allows you to dream of extravagance in a world full of cold modernism and soulless grotesque typefaces.

Classification
Display

Styles
Regular

Release
2019

Contact
janiksandbothe.de
@janiksandbothe

EUPHORIA

Everett
Nolan Paparelli

Everett originated during Nolan Paparelli's studies at the ECAL/
University of Art & Design Lausanne as his diploma work and has
evolved ever since. Initially inspired by the work of the American
photographer Daniel Everett, it quickly became more personal and
resulted in his own take on the grotesque genre. The font's
symmetrical structure is balanced with an organic drawing and a
particular digital flavor. Strong typographic details add a high
tension while keeping a reading comfort, finding the right balance
between a font that is graphic yet fluid. Low ascenders and
descenders allow designers to set text with tight line spacing, resulting in economizing space. The fonts are fully equipped with various
stylistic sets, ligatures and case-sensitive forms among other features.
The weights, ranging from Hairline to Super with corresponding
Italics, form a cohesive and versatile family offering various design
solutions from book to poster design, from branding to signage
systems and much more.

Classification
Neogrotesk

Styles

Hairline	**Book**	**Super**
Thin	**Medium**	**+ Italics**
Ultralight	**Bold**	
Light	**Extrabold**	
Regular	**Black**	

Release
2021

Contact
nolan-paparelli.ch
@nolan_paparelli

106pt

settings in points
units percent
degrees

TWK
Everett
...per

OTF
(CFF)
TWK®

v3.000
Glyphs 2.6.7
build 1355

Leading

128pt

Vertical
offset

Tilt

0pt 0°

TWK
Everett
Extrabold

OTF
(CFF)
TWK®

v3.000
Glyphs 2.6.7
build 1355

Horizontal
& vertical scale

100%

Tracking

VA -40

TWK
Everett
Medium

OTF
(CFF)
TWK®

v3.000
Glyphs 2.6.7
build 1355

Kerning

Metric

'21 18 00 UTC+1   CH-TWK SPECIMEN
IM⁵   JC ᵂ
EVERETT   NOLAN   UNTITLED   DANIEL
TYPEFACE   PAPARELLI   PICTURE   EVERETT

21 ... 00 UTC+1   CH ...
NP ... JC ᵂ
TYPE MELTEN...

Eyes
Marie Ducrocq

Eyes was originally created for a publication of the same name, which is a collection of images of politicians that all wear the same kind of thin metal glasses. I was looking for an impactful and unexpected typeface to design the cover of the book, and as I couldn't find one that made me think of eyes, I decided I would draw it. The base design of the letters is an oval outer shape based on the shape of an eye, which made it a real challenge to design legible and well-balanced characters. This results in a very high contrasted typeface with geometrical oval-shaped counters.

Classification
Display

Styles
Regular

Release
2019

Contact
marieducrocq.com
@p__lumm

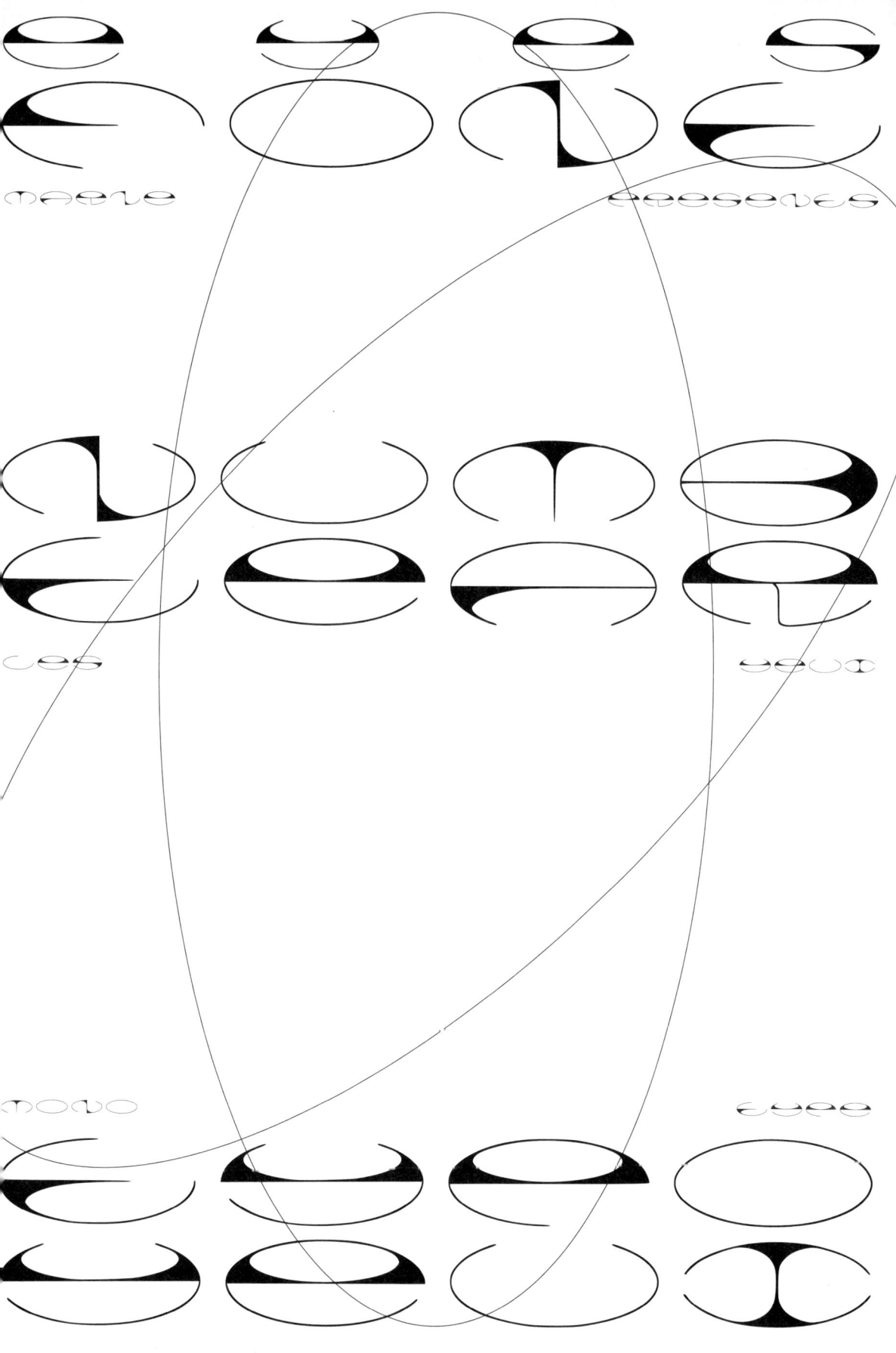

Felsen
Thomas Maier

The concept of the font is generated randomness. Using the Python programming language and UFO format, a font was created that produces interesting effects in its details due to randomly generated values. There are weight changes, corners and gaps within the characters, as well as very large and small spaces between them. The strict set of programmed rules meets randomness and creative decision-making.

Therefore the typeface acquires an exceptionally unique, eye-catching appearance. Each time the font is exported, chance produces a new and altered result. These variations are reflected within the OpenType features in the form of multiple glyphs per character. Due to the generative quality, many font styles could be created. The idea for the typeface was born many years ago in a seminar with three weights and an extremely limited number of characters. In 2023, the typeface will be expanded to 167 characters and published.

Classification
Gothic

Styles

Thin	**Semibold**
Extralight	**Bold**
Light, Book	**Extrabold**
Regular	**Black**
Medium	

Release
2023

Contact
thomasmaier.design
@thomasmaier

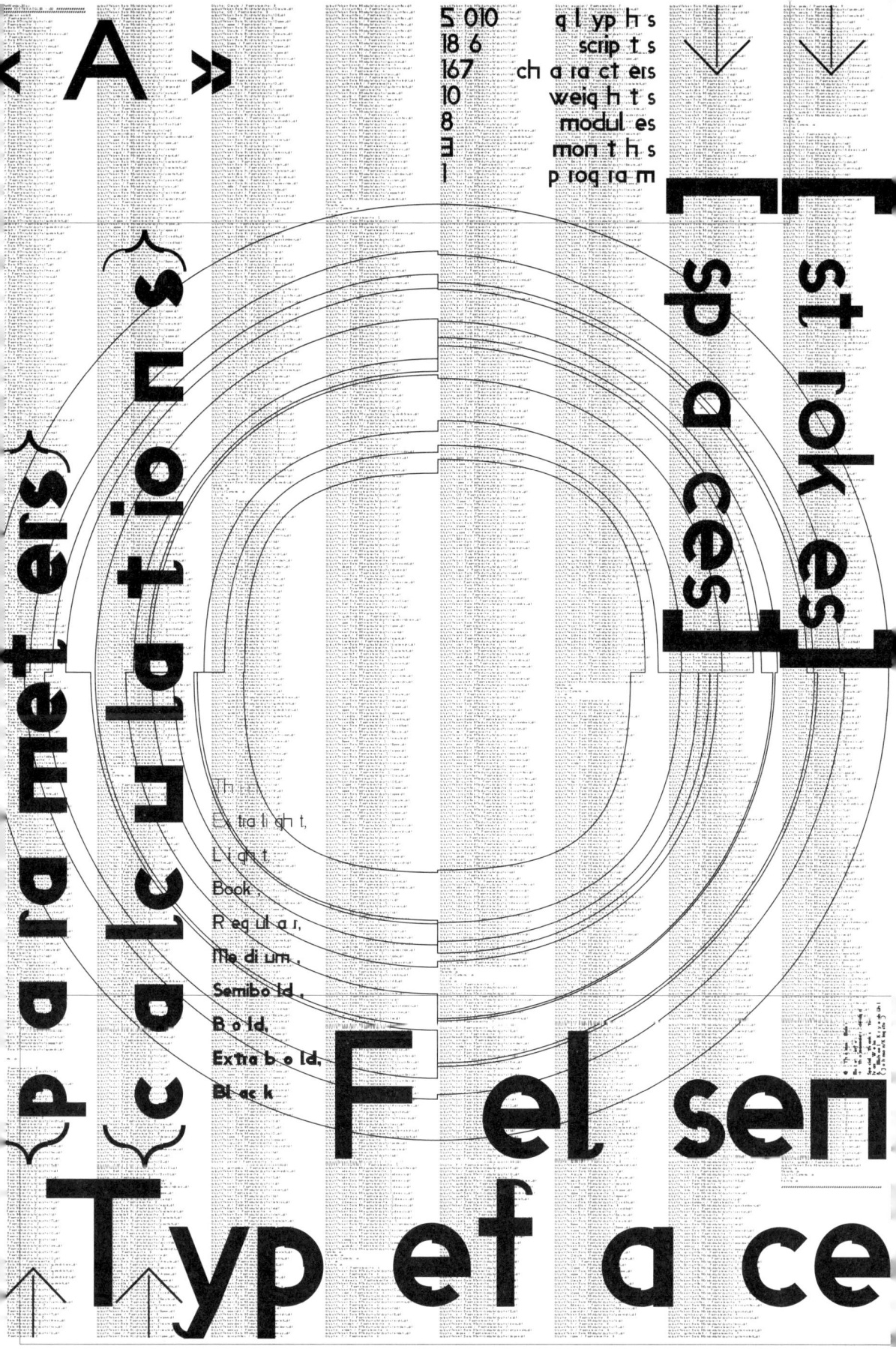

‹ A ›

5 010   glyphs
186   scripts
167   characters
10   weights
8   modules
3   months
1   program

{parameters}
(calculations)

[spaces]

[strokes]

Thin,
Extralight,
Light,
Book,
Regular,
Medium,
Semibold,
Bold,
Extrabold,
Black

Felsen

Typeface

Gammadion
Laurent Peteuil

Gammadion is a font inspired by Hellenistic design. The concept driving this project was to develop a monolinear and geometric alphabet that strikes a balance between the aesthetic patterns of ancient Greece and certain modern typefaces, such as the Neue Alphabet. During my master's degree my interest in ancient European aesthetics compelled me to create related designs. I had a plethora of beautiful books from that era, replete with exquisite heliogravure printed images of items, statues, pottery, landscapes, and more. I aspired to craft an alphabet drawing inspiration from these aesthetics, albeit in a minimalist fashion, reminiscent of Wim Crouwel's New Alphabet—something essential. I was drawn to the way its minimal and geometrical design, in tandem with compositional choices, transforms the letters into an abstract pattern. Text resembles poetry or embroidery, composed in a deliberate manner for a specific purpose that can encompass both meaning and aesthetics.

Classification
Sans Serif

Styles
Minimal
Monolinear

Release
2017

Contact
laurentpeteuil.fr

Gig
Franziska Weitgruber

Gig is an expressive display typeface with roots in felt pen writing, taking aspects of sign painting-style letter shapes. The design can be seen as a contemporary, indirect quote of different eras of lettering and typefaces derived from a flat tool and a visible writing gesture, such as Charles Loupot's lettering for St. Raphaël (1938), Banco by Roger Excoffon (1951), or examples of American advertising from the 1950s. At the same time, Gig is a personal exploration of the writing gesture and speed. Originally developed with the purpose of music events and publications in mind, Gig is suitable for many different display applications.

Classification
Script
Display

Styles
Thin
Light
Regular
Semibold
Bold

Release
2018

Contact
franziskaweitgruber.com
@franziskaweit

sleeping we

no paranoi

no paranoi

careful to u

careful to a

never wash

leeping we

no paranoi

Golgotha
Rafael Ribas

Golgotha is a revival typeface from a 19th century classic fantasy face specimen by Renault & Marcou. I only had a sample of a few capital letters and then developed the high x-height lowercases and an alternate set of larger capitals, to be used as initials or simply as alternates. The task was to keep particularities and find a spirit in the original sample, while trying to actualize the forms.

Classification
Classic Fantasy

Styles
Atlas (straight)
Axis (oblique)

Release
2016

Contact
rafaelribas.com
@3nc9re

FRANZ LISZT CLAUDE DEBUSSY
CAMILLE SAINT-SAENS
MODESTE MOUSSORGSKY
ANTONIN DVORAK GUSTAV HOLST
VASSILY KALINIKOV CÉSAR CUI
EDUARD NAPRAVNIK
CARL TAUSIG ARRIGO BOITO
SERGE TANEYEV PAUL PABST
RUGGERO LEONCAVALLO
LUDWIG THUILLE AUGUST ENNA
ARNOLD BAX PIETRO MASCAGNI
RICCARDO ZANDONAI

AVRIL/MAI 2018

GoliaGolia
Alex Valentina

GoliaGolia was born from the desire to create something with a modern look but maintaining some kind of classic baroque traits. Each letter has been designed to have distinct details that differ from the rest of the letters while still being able to fit in the whole style of the font. It has been designed keeping a handwriting feeling in order to make it geometrically imperfect. This creates a less rigid type in which the inexact hand lines meet with modern sharp display curves. This gives spirit and an uncommon contrast to the typeface. As It's Nice That described it: "A spaceship collided with a baroque cathedral."
I can't agree more.

Classification
Experimental Serif

Styles
GoliaGolia Regular
GoliaGolia Sharp

Release
2019

Contact
alexvalentina.com
@alexvxvxvxvx

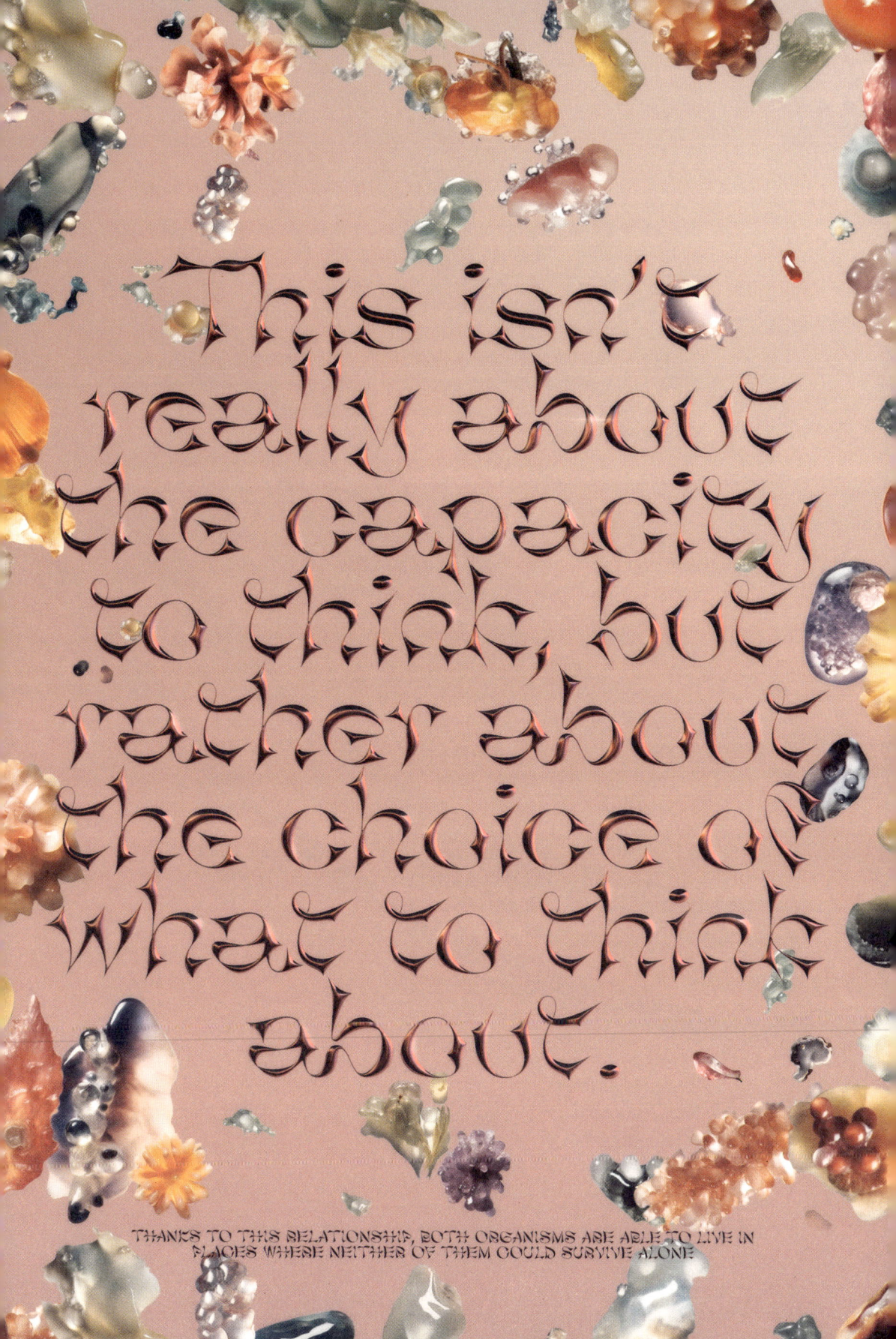

This isn't really about the capacity to think, but rather about the choice of what to think about.

THANKS TO THIS RELATIONSHIP, BOTH ORGANISMS ARE ABLE TO LIVE IN PLACES WHERE NEITHER OF THEM COULD SURVIVE ALONE

Gradial
Lena Weber

Gradial is a modular system. Its legibility is not created by shape, but by the transitions between light and dark. The shape of the glyphs is not concrete but lies much more in the in-betweens. It is able to tile any surface with zero gaps and recoloring the gradients can create several effects: glossy, metallic, shadowed, glowing, and more. Gradial supports variable outlines as well as variable gradients, making it one of the first typefaces to combine these features via the Colorv1 format. It uses this combination to achieve its second special feature: Variable encryption.

The gradient stripes are shifted and warped, so the legibility of the glyphs continuously disappears. There are two different styles of warping: Random and Ordered. In addition to these experimental axes, there are also variable widths and italics. The recoloring and axial shifting in combination with animation allow headlines and visuals to shine in a wide variety of eye-catching variations.

Classification
Experimental

Styles

Mono	Variable Axes:	Custom Colour-Effect
Regular	Random Encryption	
Italic	Ordered Encryption	
Encrypted	Italic	
	Width	

Release
2022

Contact
lenaweber.com
@lenaweber404

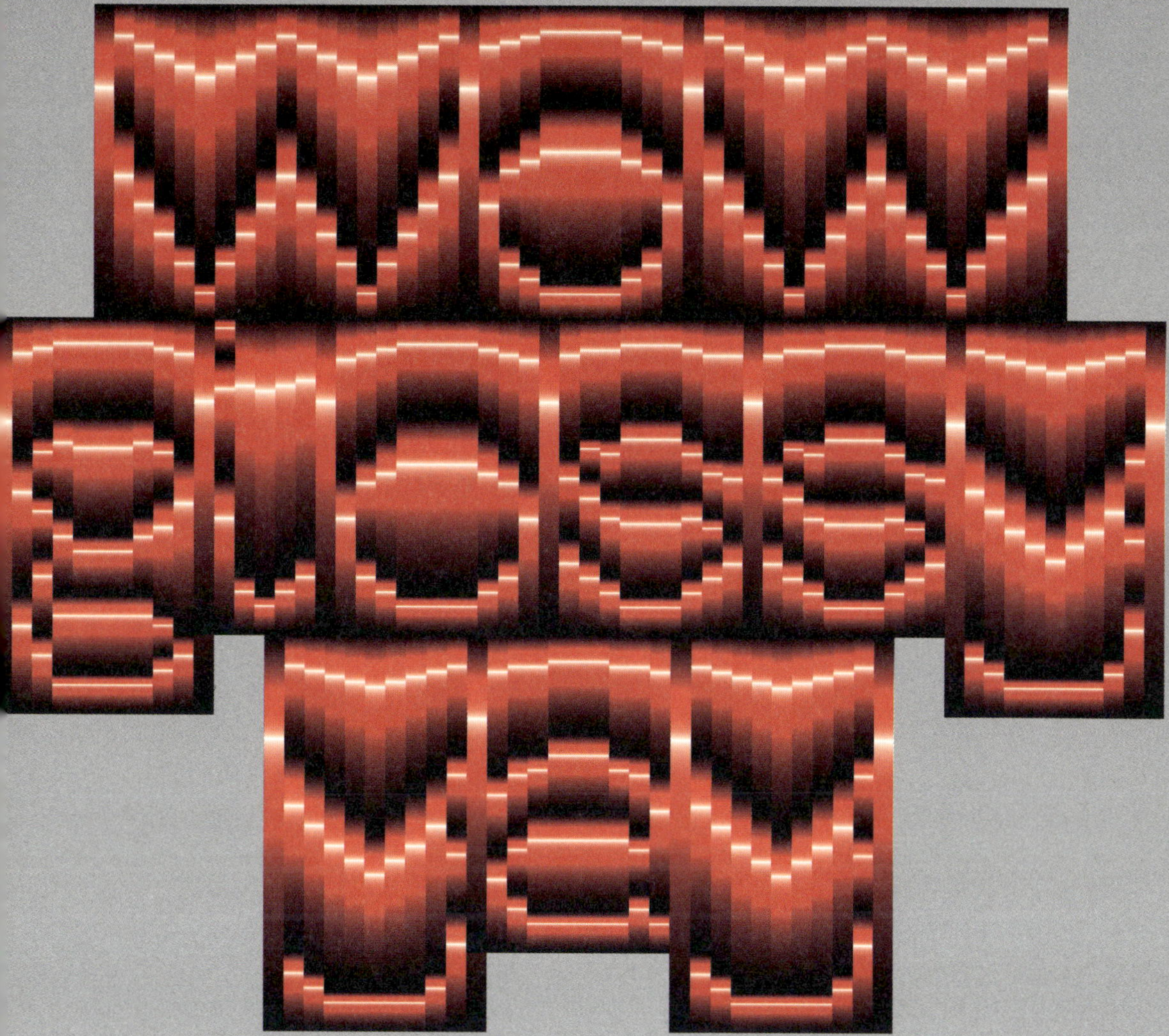

Grand Slang
Nikolas Wrobel

Grand Slang is a new font, boldly discovering and reshaping the essence of the beautiful American, mid-20th century calligraphy. The inescapable desire not only to recreate but to retranslate historic letterforms led to the creation of a very own, sleek and reduced Grand Slang.

Passing on the beauty and warmth of the former hands of Oscar Ogg and William A. Dwiggins, Grand Slang comes with an idealistic vision, merging Grotesk and Serif together in over 310 individually, non-modular crafted uppercase letters, ligatures, figures, and signs.

Classification
Serif

Styles
Roman
Italic
B-Side

Release
2019

Contact
nikolastype.com
@nikolastype

Gray Zone
Youl Joe, Heejae Yang

Gray Zone is a typeface created by folding paper strips so that the front and back intersect. It represents a hybrid concept of black and white, duality, and uncertainty. It symbolizes the midpoint between positivity and negativity. In offset printing, gray is represented by black dots. In other words, gray is not a mixture of black and white, but rather a group of black. We need time to make any choice, and sometimes the decision ends up being a combination of choice and non-choice (reservation). Therefore, the time period is bound to remain in a gray zone.

Classification
Display

Styles
N/A

Release
2023

Contact
ktowntype.com

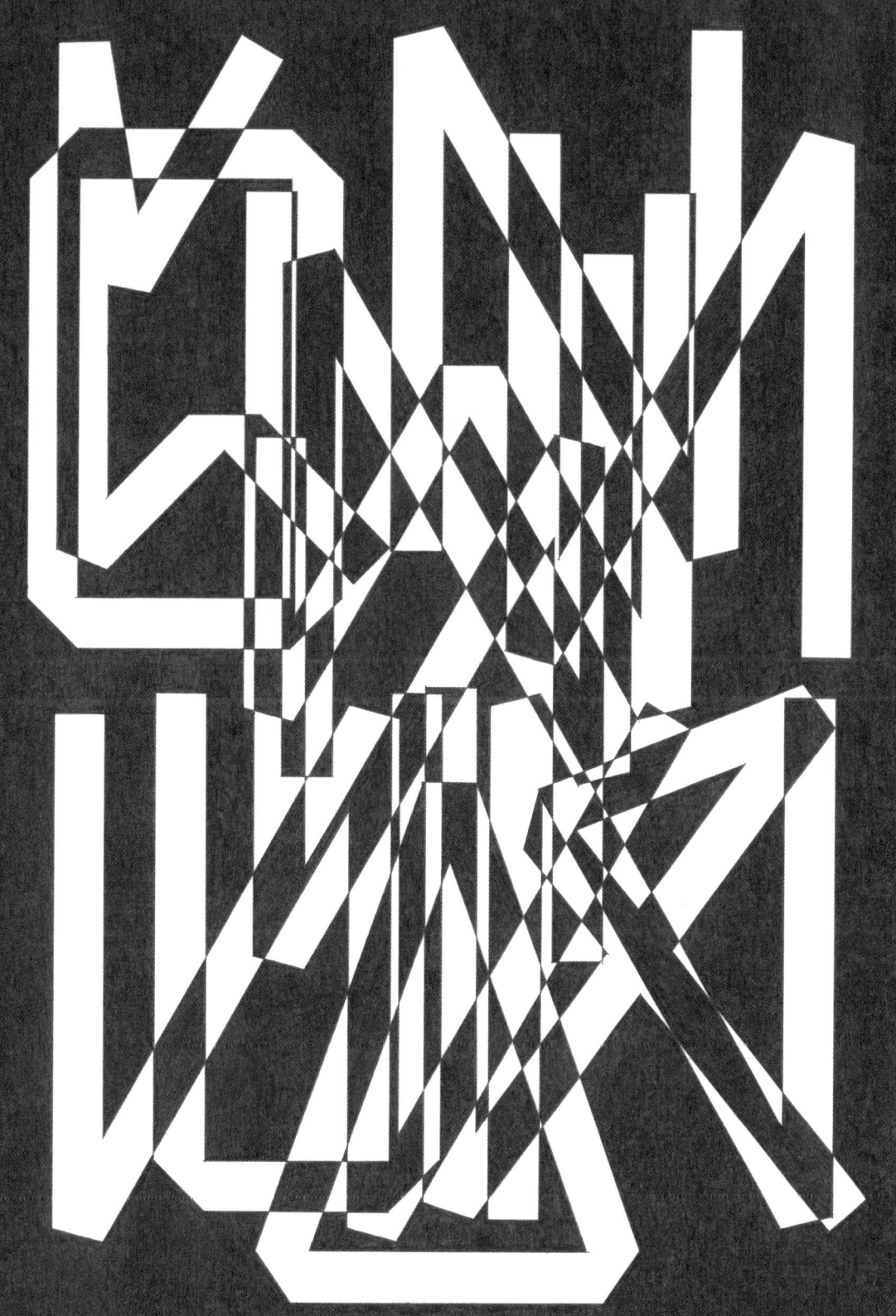

Gravita
Lena Weber

Gravita visualizes the different gravitational forces of the planets in our solar system. The ink is drawn to the corners, as if the typeface itself were affected by a gravitational force that drags the ink to the corners of the glyphs.

    The planetary cuts are generated via interpolation between Zero G (0%)—the base cut without any gravitational distortion—and Jupiter (100%), as it has the strongest gravitational pull of all the planets. Home represents Earth's gravitational pull.

    Gravita is in development and being reworked as a variable font. As an experimental display project, it serves as both a typeface and an infographic.

Classification
Sans Serif
Display

Styles

Zero G	Moon	Variable Axis
Mercury	Jupiter	Gravitational Pull
Mars	Saturn	
Venus	Uranus	
Home	Neptune	

Release
2018

Contact
lenaweber.com
@lenaweber404

Grotesk Grotesk
Armin Roth, Simon Bork, Lukas Betzler (studio panorama)

The Grotesk Grotesk was designed in 2017 for the Kunsthochschule Mainz. Its expressive and experimental feel describes processual artistic work, breaking through learned conventions and questioning artistic practice to explore new possibilities. The typeface contains four alternate letter variants for each letter, whereby the individual variants are loaded randomly and the respective letter cannot be influenced by the user—the typeface combines itself on its own. The bulky impression creates a strong recognition and enables the art academy to create a branding that is based on concise typography only.

Classification
Constructed Grotesk

Styles
N/A

Release
2017

Contact
studiopanorama.de
@roth_armin
@studiopanorama.de

GELD HOCH HÄNDE RAUS

Güggeli
Fabio Biesel

Güggeli is a slightly slanted Sans Serif typeface. The goal was to create a contemporary typeface with some unique and slanted letterforms, based on the principle of unawareness. The inspiration for Güggeli came during a trip through Denmark. After seeing a house that was totally crooked and lopsided between two very modern, straight houses, I fell in love with it. I loved this surprising effect. This contrast. Based on this feeling, I designed Güggeli. By the way, the name means fried chicken in Switzerland. I just chose it because I think it sounds great. And not so serious.

Classification
Sans Serif

Styles
Regular
Bold
Regular Rounded
Bold Rounded

Release
2018

Contact
studiofabiobiesel.com

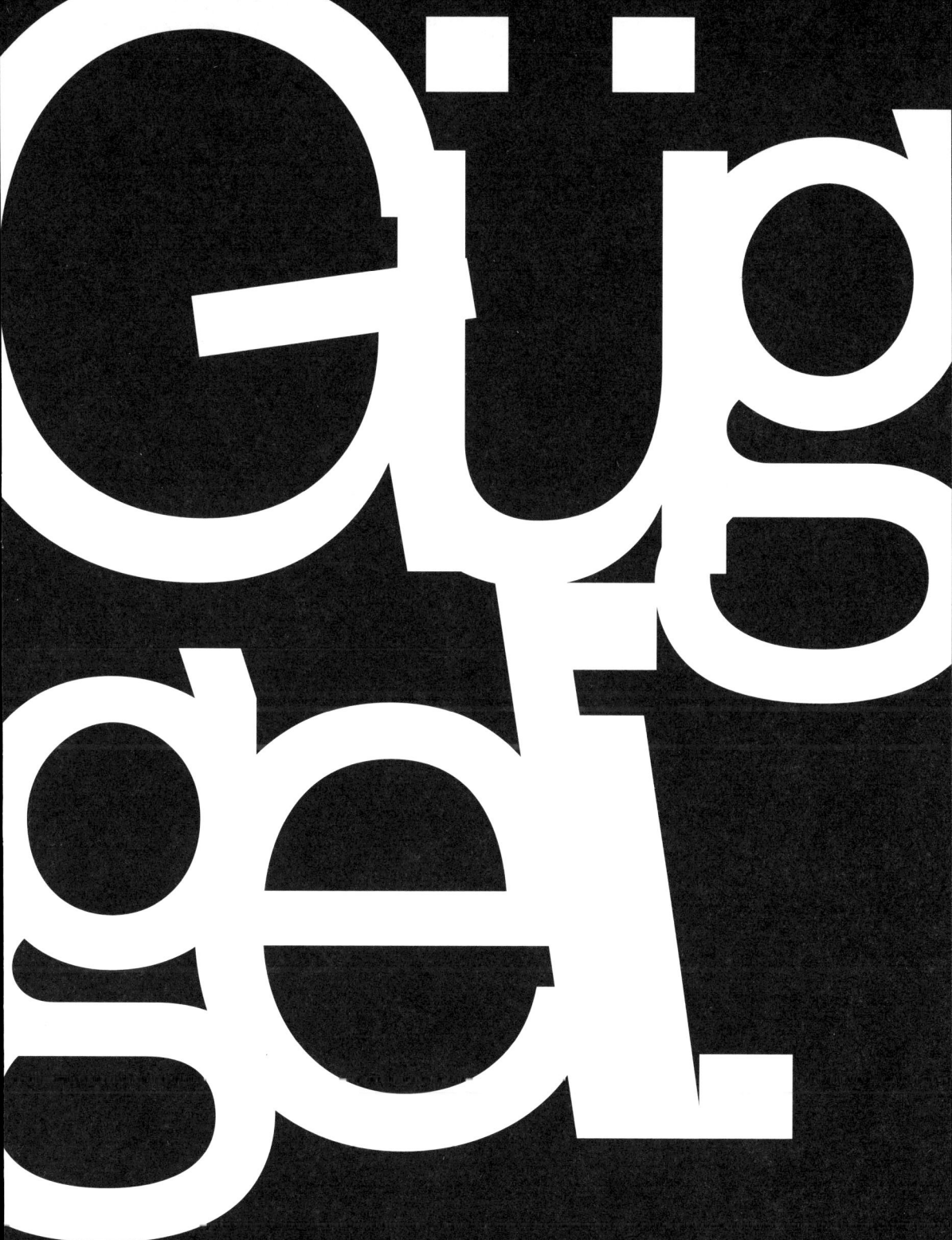

Halunke
Elena Schneider

What looks like the aura of your migraine actually started out when experimenting with geometric Arabic pattern designs. Halunke is an expressive display typeface with two styles but no curves. Available on futurefonts.xyz.

Classification
Display

Styles
Regular
Italic

Release
2019

Contact
elenaschneider.com
@elefontele

Halunke

BEFORETIMEeverythingSEVENTIETHb
ackpacked EMPATHISTS acetylated? EV
ERYTHING camelopard IMPROVISER cau
liflory. GRIDLOCKED chronology UNEX
PLORED ultradense ZINKIFYING diama
gnets EVERYTHING orbiculate & MISFOC
USED geodynamic KARABINERS improvi
ser IDENTIFIED mekometers; GRIDLOCK
ED karabiners BITUMINIZE watermelo
n BIOPHILIAS megapixels BEKNIGHTED

Heartbeats
Erik Sachse

I made this typeface while traveling through North China. The conditions were challenging, as my laptop kept shutting off. However, after finding a stable power source in the woods, I was ready to continue expanding the boundaries I had set for this font. Each glyph rendered seamlessly on my computer, and I felt a sense of unity with technology, I was immersed in the process at every step.

Classification
Script

Styles
Light
Regular
Medium
Bold
Black

Release
2018

Contact
@napoleontypefaces

Helvetica Blows
Paula Scher, Bruno Bergallo

Helvetica Blows is an alphabet that initially existed as an animation with the idea that you could create an alphabet by inflating each letter into balloon shapes. The alphabet was inspired by my personal dislike of Helvetica.

The alphabet originated from a project where the goal was to promote and celebrate Monotype's new catalog of the many weights of Helvetica, shown together from the thinnest to the fattest form. The letters were imagined as a still animation sequence of someone pumping up the thin Helvetica until it might burst.

Titled "Blowing Up Helvetica," the project consisted of three pieces—two animations and a poster—that are available as a set of NFTs as part of Monotype's first-ever digital art collection.

Classification
**Bulbous Sans Serif
Display**

Styles
N/A

Release
2022

Contact
**pentagram.com
@pentagramdesign
@brunobergallo**

Icarus
Sophia Brinkgerd

Icarus is a modern experimental display typeface that blends extremely radical curves with sharp edges, capturing rapid movements and swift changes in direction. The creative process behind Icarus prioritized minimal anchor points, resulting in broad letterforms that exude both swiftness and sharpness, with a simple, symmetrical parabola shape serving as its foundation, creating a delicate but stable frame for each letter.

This typeface, particularly its name, draws profound inspiration from Ovid's 'Metamorphoses', specifically borrowing from the dramatic tale of Daedalus and Icarus. It represents an experimental typographical interpretation of their ascent and tragic downfall, abstractly weaving the narrative through its light but forceful design.

Classification
Display

Styles
Regular

Release
2019

Contact
sophiabrinkgerd.com
@sophiabrinkgerd

Innschbruck
Daniel Stuhlpfarrer

Innschbruck is a modular display variable font. It was designed in the course of a corporate design for an Austrian graphic designer living in Berlin. The modular basic forms of the typeface developed from the graphic designer's initials. Another central aspect of the typeface is the Austrian language. The big difference in language between Austria and Germany is the stretching or lengthening of vowels and whole words. From this basis, the typefaces can be extended as a whole but also in parts, adapting to the language. To achieve this, the font was built on two masters as a variable font, allowing seamless adjustments to the pronunciation. This enables an exact visual representation of the designer's phonetic pronunciation.

Classification
Modular Display

Styles
**Regular Ultra
Condensed
Regular Extra
Condensed
Regular Condensed**

**Regular Semi
Condensed
Regular Medium
Regular Semi
Expanded**

**Regular Expanded
Regular Extra Expanded
Regular Ultra Expanded
Regular Variable**

Release
2019

Contact
**danielstuhlpfarrer.com
@daniel_stuhlpfarrer**

Italica
Sylvain Esposito

Italica is the result of a one-week workshop with Emmanuel Rey (SWTY). The premise was to create a typeface under certain conditions/ parameters (conditional design 101) that were determined by drawing lots. My challenge was to not have any horizontal paths, and I ended up sketching what I would call a straightened-up Italic typeface.

Historically, Italic typefaces are designed that way for a reason; they are based on calligraphy, which is traditionally slanted. Their function is to highlight and that's something that almost everybody knows and agrees upon—it's part of the culture.

Italica borrows from two categories with different purposes, Roman and Italic, which puts it in a kind of grey area. You don't really know what to do with it because it hijacks your internal software. But you recognize it.

Classification
Humanistic Sans Serif

Styles
Regular

Release
2015

Contact
@sylvainesposito

Italica

Sghembo

Griffo

Corsivo

Obliquo

Jako
Lisa Petersen

Language unites and separates at the same time. It is used for communication, but also for identification. Especially in times of constant occupation, the Serbian language offered a way to preserve one's own culture over this period. The script Jako (Serbian = strong, powerful) is the result of a ten-day trip to Belgrade in April 2016. It deals with the origin and development of Serbian characters.

Classification
Display

Styles
N/A

Release
2017

Contact
@peter.lise
@bureau_est

BEOGRAD

TYPEFACE JAKO

THE WHITE CITY

APRIL 2016

Jones
Mirko Borsche

At the time the office was founded in 2007, Nike asked me to do art works for an exhibition in Berlin and Munich. I didn't even have my computer set up yet, so there was no way to work digitally. So I sat in Bogenhausen with parts of my magazine archives and started to work with them. Just cutting out letters was too boring, so I worked with pictures, or rather with picture shapes that look like letters. The final artwork was 5 meters high and 16 meters long. It was a quote from NWA—so with lots of letters. Looking at it today, the typeface/font has more of an early 90s touch. That's why the typeface needs a female name. Jones, like Grace Jones, transmits just the right vibe. It was then digitized in 2023 and now you can also write in color.

Classification
Display

Styles
N/A

Release
2023

Contact
bureauborsche.com
@mirkoborsche

Keramika
Mathilde André

Keramika is a display typeface built on the shape of a ceramic amphora. Typing in Keramika sets a peculiar atmosphere, halfway between primary Mesopotamian cuneiform writing and sci-fi alien language. Keramika is research on legibility, scripture origins, and geometry. In development.

Classification
Display

Styles
Regular

Release
2018

Contact
@matildacallas
@stunningbookdesigns

SOIL

- CUNEIFORM SYMBOLS
- PERSEPOLIS
- SUMERIAN WRITING
- ALIEN

Kevin Fidèle
Isia Yurovsky

Kevin Fidèle is inspired by a French typeface from the 1890-1918 period (Belle Époque). I found a reproduction of the original font on the Museum of Printing Lyon website where the font is described as follows: "Simply named 'Fantaisie,' this astonishing typeface, resembling an italic mechanistic style with very modern curves, showcases the unrestrained creativity of 19th-century type designers." At least a century old, it possesses a contemporary flair that wouldn't necessarily exclude it from a catalog of modern digital type foundries. Personally, I was drawn to the contrast between the mechanical, elongated serifs that adorned the thin Italic structure.

Classification
French Fantaisie

Styles
Light Italic

Release
N/A

Contact
@isia_y

GINE GEARS MECHANIS
CIRCUITRY W IRES AUTO
N COMPONEN TS ASSEMBL
IBRATION CO NTROL PAN
DRAULICS PN EUMATICS L
CATION MAIN TENANCE O.
NG SYSTEM P OWER SUPH
NSORS TRANS MISSION VO.
GE PERFORMA NCE ROBOT
FICIENCY REPLICA
ENGINEERING
SSEMBLY LINE
AINTENANC
OPERATIO
PU

symphony of human ingenuity and advanced machinery, working in tandem to create everything from automobiles to consumer electronics. The factory floor hums with

n modern industrial landscapes, factories stand as the beating heart of production. These sprawling complexes are

La Nord
Raoul Gottschling

La Nord was created in search of a functional Grotesk with a lot of personality. What exactly this personality would look like slowly became apparent as the design process progressed. What was clear, however, was that the balance between personality and usability should be maintained. La Nord runs a little further than Grotesk fonts normally do, and the x-height is also a little larger. In addition to the proportions, the shapes of the font also aim to create character through details. The line contrast is higher than that of a pure Grotesk; on the shoulders and edges of some letters (r, g, a, etc.) it even resembles the contrast of a serif font.

Classification
Neo Grotesk

Styles
Light
Semi Light
Regular
Medium
Bold

Release
2018

Contact
raoulgottschling.de
@raoulgottschling

Heavy Water

en torrent the of water rips makes its are way down in from the full Seignosse flow, tewater maelstrom to the beach north.

Langulaire
Loris Pernoux

Langulaire is a display typeface that has been designed with contrasting curves blended with a minimum of one ninety-degree angle for each character. It is ideally suited for medium and large-scale use: the bigger it is, the more the shapes suggest an abstract result, as when characters are isolated. I drew a first version of Langulaire during my graphic design studies at the Gerrit Rietveld Academie. I then developed and released it a few months after graduating. Langulaire stems from a simple idea: to design a typography as an image that is only legible to those who take the time to read it. Nowadays, we consume a lot of images every day—take social media, for instance. It requires time and patience to learn to read and understand Langulaire. I was inspired by the images at the basis of hieroglyphics, graffiti, and calligraphy. I tried to situate my design somewhere in between those things and create letterforms that need to be deciphered, that are deceptively suggestive of a new language, and challenge the reader to a more pictorial mode of expression.

Classification
Display

Styles
N/A

Release
2017

Contact
lorispernoux.fr
@loris_pernoux

Lapicide
Emilie Vizcano

Introducing Lapicide, a serif typeface that draws inspiration from the art of stone engraving and the skillful craftsmanship of stone-cutters. The name "Lapicide" encompasses both the stone engraving technique and the resulting masterpiece it produces. The typeface captures the essence of inscriptions meticulously carved into architectural elements and monuments, known specifically as lapidary inscriptions. With distinct serifs and unique, chiseled-looking terminals, Lapicide replicates the effect of engraved typography on stone surfaces. The typeface evokes a sense of timelessness and reverence, harkening back to the rich history of stone carving and the enduring legacy of inscriptions left for generations to come. Lapicide is a tribute to the ancient art of engraving and a versatile font choice that brings an air of refined elegance, be it in print or digital media.

Classification
Old Style

Styles
Light

Release
2019

Contact
emilievizcano.com
@emilievizcano

LAPICIDE

miracle
quicksilver

240g   2019

Lausanne
Nizar Kazan

Lausanne is an extraordinarily sophisticated sans-serif font with an ultra-organic aesthetic, very legible in small sizes and full of refined details in display sizes. First of all, it was designed with the intention of responding to the historical sans-serif like Helvetica. Lausanne brings to this intention the peculiarities of digital typography. For example, the duality and versatility of a text and a display character. In addition, the ascending and descending lines are very short and give a compact appearance to this character.

To date, the Lausanne 300 has been used by many designers for MoMA (USA), mono GmbH (Germany), Playboy Magazine, AFTRS (Australia), Landesmuseum Zurich or Universal Music. The complete family will be available in 20 weights (50 to 1000) at Weltanschauung 2023.

Classification
Grotesk

Styles
**50, 100, 150, 200...
to 1000**

Release
2017

Contact
**nizarkazan.ch
@nizarkazan**

Lil Thug
Brando Corradini

The Lil Thug typeface is an angular-shaped typeface, belonging to the sans-serif classification, which has a striking diamond-shaped dot inserted inside and outside some letters. The poster is made only from typographic characters where letters and numbers have been inserted, the latter hidden by horizontal lines which represent the lines of time. The dates at the bottom, hidden by the central shape, are the ones in which I created the typeface (2017), the publication of the New Aesthetic 1 (2019), and finally the date that corresponds to this remastered publication. Lil Thug typeface was created by me in 2018, inspired by the figure of rapper Lil Peep who died prematurely and tragically from an overdose at the age of 21.

Classification
Sans Serif

Styles
Regular

Release
2017

Contact
brandocorradini.com
@brando.corradini

Line
Sepus Noordmans (Parabol Studio)

Line is an odd reverse-contrast display typeface that goes beyond mere inspiration from 1960s and 1970s record covers. It delves deep into the visual culture of that revolutionary era, capturing the essence and the feeling of wearing vintage fashion, watching dusty wallpapers, eye-catching elegant shapes on cars and its aesthetics, or dreading bold film titles. This typeface isn't just a nod to the past; it's a small study of the entire spectrum of its time. By seamlessly merging nostalgia with modern sophistication, Line manages to evoke the spirit of a bygone era while injecting a fresh and bold contemporary touch into every detail.

Classification
Display
Reverse Contrast

Styles
Bold
Demibold
Regular
Light
Extralight

Release
2017

Contact
parabolstudio.no
@sepusnoordmans

LLUNA
Sara Bastai

LLUNA is an experimental display typeface created in 2018. Developed while I was studying and practicing graphic design but also already navigating through different fields. It came as an opportunity to experiment without any constraints or goals. Nevertheless, there was an excitement around it to expand to diverse mediums, such as garments and ultimately to create visuals for it. LLUNA emerged from a deliberate exercise of shapes. Shapes that were inspired and took form from lunar silhouettes. Smooth curves contrasted with thin angles. A sort of semi-italic font that achieves balanced contrasts and shapes, striving to evoke a legendary and robust spirit.

Classification
Script

Styles
N/A

Release
2018

Contact
sarabastai.com
@sarabastai

MD Maya
Moby Digg

The interdisciplinary festival Panama Plus tries to create a utopian world in which its visitors head for an alternative experience and (hopefully) forget in which reality they are currently in. We wanted to create a font that could embody this mentality and remind of a hidden civilization. The symbols of the typography somehow form signs but could also be the silhouette of a building, a mark in a cave. With a big set of alternate characters for almost every letter, we embraced the diversity of the festival and tried to build bridges between cultures and societies.

Classification
Display

Styles
Regular

Release
2017

Contact
mobydigg.de
@mobydigg

Mercial
Luca Pellegrini

While browsing my favorite thrift store, I stumbled upon a pile of free VHS tapes. One cassette, hand-labeled "Flight of the Navigator," immediately caught my eye. After converting it to digital, I intended to enjoy a nostalgic movie night. However, exhaustion led me to fall asleep before the film's end. Upon waking up, I found the movie re-placed by an infomercial. A charismatic figure offered to foretell my future. Lucky numbers: 1, 12, 23, 34, 6, and 18. Intriguingly, the infomercial showcased a tightly spaced serif font, reminiscent of print ads of the period rather than the usual fonts appearing on TV. My curiosity about the font led to a dead-end search. Therefore, I decided to create my own version and that's how Mercial came to be. Aiming to pay homage to the place where I found these letters, I decided to make my own infomercial. The idea was also to produce a playful parody of the typical way of selling fonts today, where every font claims to be the best for this or that purpose. Mercial shines in text sizes while offering intriguing details when displayed in larger formats.

Classification
Serif Transitional (A. Novarese)

Styles
Regular
Medium
Bold

Release
2019

Contact
@lcpllgrn

Mercial

Ladies and gentlemen, gather around and prepare to embark on a whimsical journey through the magical world of Mercial font. Brace yourselves because this isn't just a font; it's like a font on a jeweled rollercoaster ride through realms of elegance and fun. Imagine this: You're on a quest to design an invitation for your pet parrot's tea party and want it to be nothing short of extraordinary. Mercial swoops in, turning your feathered fiesta into a spectacle of serifs! Watch

as Polly sips her tea together for a tea time so refined the Queen's corgis would be impressed. But hold onto your top hats because there's an encore! Are you tired of your mundane shopping lists looking as exciting as a loaf of plain bread? With Mercial, your lists become an epic quest, and your reminders read like lines of Shakespearean drama. "To buy or not to purchase, that is the essential dilemma!" Ever felt like declaring your love to your morning cup of joe, that lovely potion of dawn? Mercial takes your hearted confessions to newfound clarity! "My dearest Coffee, you dote upon my soul, and you complete me! You understand me like a caffeinated sonnet when the midnight snack cravings come knocking, Mercial transforms your snack inventory into a gourmet masterpiece. "Savory Nacho Chips - A symphony of crunch and cheese, fit for a connoisseur!" Your snacks have never sounded so posh! But there's more, my friends! Mercial font isn't just about flamboyant creativity; it's also a font that's incredibly versatile in text size. Your business reports will exude professionalism and

essays will shine brighter than a supernova, your messages will become literature. You could rival the classics! Colleagues will marvel at your textual prowess! But wait, there's more! Mercial font doesn't stop at English; it's a font that dabbles in foreign languages with uncommon accents. Want to write a love letter in French but can't quite nail that accent? Mercial font turns your heartfelt notes into a melodious symphony of umlauts and consonants! "Meister Kaffee, du bist meine Sonne am Morgen!" So why confine yourself to the ordinary when you can embrace the extraordinary with Mercial font? It's not just a font; it's a font-tastic adventure filled with laughter, love, and a touch of extravagance. Dive into the creativity and versatility of Mercial Font today, and let your own projects soar to new levels of hilarity. Don't miss out on fantastic fun - get Mercial font and experience the typeface revolution of our time! Imagine this: You're tasked with designing a birthday card for your pet rock, Rocky Balboa, and you want it to be a rock-solid masterpiece. Mercial font comes to the rescue, turning your rocky card into a stone-cold symphony of razzmatazz as Rocky himself would marvel about his newfound sophistication. But that's just the tip of the iceberg! Sick of your daily to-do lists looking as exciting as watching paint dry? With Mercial, your mundane tasks become epic quests, and your reminders read like lines of Shakespearean drama. "To take out the trash or not to take out trash, that is the age-old question!" Ever felt like expressing your undying love to your cozy blanket? Mercial can turn your affectionate musings into an epic of comfort and warmth. "Oh, blanket, why embrace dost thou, thy softness cradles

Messapia
Luca Marsano (Collletttivo)

Messapia is an experimental type family composed of two—seemingly unrelated—styles: Regular, inspired by an old 19th-century typeface, and Bold, a heavy humanist extended face. The project was born with the singular concept to create an unconventional family.
I combined and compared two very different designs from different eras to put them into dialogue. I tried to standardize proportions and contrast and the result is a font with two very different styles sharing one matrix. This makes it versatile in creating interesting layouts because they complement each other or can be interchanged.
An intermediate weight was also planned which would have been the result of an interpolation of bot—but it never saw the light of day :)
Messapia is an open-source licensed font and is part of the Collletttivo type foundry catalog, so it can be downloaded freely, and expanded and modified.

Classification
Serif
Sans Serif

Styles
Regular
Bold

Release
2019

Contact
shuluq.com
collletttivo.it
@_shuluq
@collletttivo

MEDEA & GIASONE

(72pt)
(Bold)

Pharmakón
(Bold)

Corinto

Vello d'oro

Glauce

Euripide

Iolco

Egeo

(Reg)

(1865) Gustave Moreau
(Reg)

485B.C. — 406B.C.
(Reg)

Argo
(Reg)

Mihara
Kia Tasbihgou

Mihara was drawn as an extension of a sign I saw from the Mihara train station platform in early June 2018. It was on the front of a building that looked like a shopping center (which is now, according to Google Translate, the "Mihara City Volunteer/Citizen Activity Support Center"), called "Paircity Mihara". The sign seems to have been taken down between the dates of November 2018 and November 2020. Given that the lettering already existed, I approached the task of extending the lettering into a full type family in a traditional manner: establish or acknowledge any rule that appears to be dictating the appearance and function of the lettering. By observing these rules, new characters can be drawn without direct source material, and the single weight can be expanded upon more straightforwardly and earnestly.

Classification
Modular Display

Styles
Mihara	**Mihara Condensed X**	**Mihara Narrow Y**
Mihara X	**Mihara Condensed Y**	**Mihara Narrow XY**
Mihara Y	**Mihara Condensed XY**	
Mihara XY	**Mihara Narrow**	
Mihara Condensed	**Mihara Narrow X**	

Release
2018

Contact
kiatas.me
@kiatas

Modal
Stefanie Vogl

Modal was originally created in 2018 for TUNICA magazine's 7th issue "Extended Fantasy". The idea behind Modal Mix was to combine two different font styles into one. Uppercase letters on the keyboard are assigned to the technical style of the typeface, and lowercase letters can be used for a more dynamic and curvy style. My main goal was to create a font that allows people to experiment and have fun during the layout process. The typeface Modal Mix contains only uppercase letters. After finishing Modal Mix (2018), I created Modal Regular (2019). This style contains both uppercase and lowercase letters in a curvy style. While Modal Mix has fewer letters, Modal Regular contains a larger amount suitable for Central Europe. Both Modal Mix and Regular are most suitable for larger font sizes and can be used with less spacing between the letters.

Classification
Display

Styles
Modal Mix
Modal Regular

Release
2019

Contact
@omfdofficial

Molodoy
Tatjana Pöschke

Molodoy is a striking font that challenges visual habits by embracing extreme contrasts. It's a reverse-contrast typeface that plays with edgy and soft shapes, as well as high distinction in line-width. Molodoy's stylistic alternatives allow control over the feel of the text, shifting it to more sharp or rounded shapes. Additionally, punctuation can be changed to provide subtle support or make a bold statement. It is a powerful and loud typeface for headlines, nevertheless lending an electrifying vibe to body text. It comes in two weights, covering West-European character sets. The word Molodoy derives from the fictional language Nadsat and means "youth," hinting towards the dualistic personality within the characters—making Molodoy both soft and a bully at the same time.

Classification
Reverse Contrast

Styles
Regular
Bold

Release
2017

Contact
www.tatipoeschke.de
@tatjana_poeschke

Ich konnte fühlen, wie die Messer in der alten Moloko zu pieken anfingen, und nun war ich bereit für ein bißchen Horrorshow. Also japste ich:

→ → → → → → → →

RAUS! RAUS! RAUS! RAUS! RAUS!

x x x

Die Nacht ist noch jung!

A A

Molodoy = [Jugendlich, jung]

Nachdem du die alte Moloko getrunken hast, liegst du so rum. Und du bist wie hypnotisiert von deinem Stiefel oder von einem Fingernagel oder was immer es sein mag.

und zur gleichen Zeit fühlst du dich am alten Kragen gepackt und geschüttelt wie eine Katze. Du wirst geschüttelt und geschüttelt, bis nichts übrig ist.

Nachdem du die alte Moloko getrunken hast, liegst du so rum. Und du bist wie hypnotisiert von deinem Stiefel oder von einem Fingernagel oder was immer es sein mag.

und zur gleichen Zeit fühlst du dich am alten Kragen gepackt und geschüttelt wie eine Katze. Du wirst geschüttelt und geschüttelt, bis nichts übrig ist.

Oh! Oh!

Moscou U.R.
Bilal Sebei

Moscou U.R. (for utopia and reality) is a font inspired by Soviet architecture and more precisely by the avant-garde period of the 1920s.

It is characterized by a rigid geometric construction that highlights the constructive elements of the letters. Each letter is thought of as an autonomous structure by a process of module deconstruction. The typeface is envisioned in two stroke weights, with the thinnest supporting the balance of the different parts of the letters.

The typeface includes key elements of the architectural avant-garde such as highlighting contrasts, the opposition of circles to linear strokes, and the desire to use asymmetry.

Classification
Lineal Geometric

Styles
Regular

Release
2015

Contact
www.bilalsebei.com
@bilal.sebei

...dyne...que d'une révolution p...
...le...s grâce à son histoir...
...sur...ne...dimension abstraite la...
...ême...Ce...'est qu'un des parado...
...e ru...ture...ue la société secrète...
...ssurant et assumant ainsi sa propre continuit...
révolutionnaires d'antan oubliaient l'implicati...
l'environnement sur leur action: ainsi a-t-on...
...des ruptures successives dans un même cadr...
construit, ce qui demandait de la part des con...
...e révolutions un effort d'imagination peu co...
C'est une des contradictions «historiques» de...
...évolutions de toujours: les monuments à la gl...
...évolutions ont été érigés a posteriori; mais le...
«opérationnel» des révolutions contemporain...
...cause directement le contexte construit! La Ré...
l'Octobre après avoir assumé le pouvoir, dev...
...us les intellectuels un symbole de renouveau

La dynamique d'une révolution po... dans le temps grâce à son histoire... assure une dimension abstraite fac... même. Ce n'est qu'un des paradox... de rupture que la société secrète p... assurant et assumant ainsi sa prop... révolutionnaires d'antan oubliaien... l'environnement sur leur action: a... à des ruptures successives dans un... construit, ce qui demandait de la... de révolutions un effort d'imagina... C'est une des contradictions «hist... révolutions de toujours: les monu... des révolutions ont été érigés a po... le caractère «opérationnel» des ré... contemporaines met en cause dire... construit! La Révolution d'Octobre... assumé le pouvoir, devient pour to... un symbole de renouveau et de lib... Rarement d'ailleurs, une révolutio... assimilée par les créateurs. Le résu... attendre: en peinture et en littérat... et en musique, en sculpture, enfin... urbanisme, le soulèvement amena... conceptuels profonds, efficaces. O... une idéologie! La dynamique d'un... politique s'inscrit dans le temps gr... propre, ce qui lui assure une dime... à l'histoire elle-même. Ce n'est qu... des moments de rupture que la soc... périodiquement, assurant et assur... continuité. Les révolutionnaires d'... l'implication de l'environnement s...

DANS LA MACHINE, RIEN N'EST SUPERFLU, ACCIDENTEL OU «DÉCORATIF». DANS LA MACHINE, RIEN NE PEUT ÊTRE AJOUTÉ OU ENLEVÉ, SOUS PEINE DE DÉTRUIRE L'ENSEMBLE. LA MACHINE EST, PAR ESSENCE, L'EXPRESSION LA PLUS PRÉCISE ET LA PLUS HARMONIEUSE DE L'IDÉAL CRÉATEUR...» MOISEI GUINZBOURG — 1924

ILYA GOLOSSOV
MOISEI GUINZBOURG
IVAN LEONIDOV

LENINGRADSKAYA
PRAVDA
GARAGE INTOURIST
INSTITUT LÉNINE

GUEORGUI KROUTIKOV
LAZAR LISSITZKY
KONSTANTIN MELNIKOV
NIKOLAI LADOVSKY

Mue
Fabian Fohrer

Mue is an experimental modular display typeface, characterized by the fusion of straight lines, perfect circles, and elongated curves. The combination of a rigid range of options—bold straight lines, mono-lined circles, high contrasted curves, and stretched dots—creates an unexpected and diversified character set. Constructed by a limited set of shapes, it challenges constraints and questions the pre-defined notion of what visual appearance a letter should take on. The typeface has three subfamilies: Mue A (mono-linear), Mue B (high-contrasted), and Mue C (inverted).

Classification
Display

Styles

Mue A Light	**Mue C Bold**
Mue A Bold	
Mue B Light	
Mue B Bold	
Mue C Light	

Release
2019

Contact
fabianfohrer.com
@fabianfohrer

Muti Anlo sse Yosh Urmu ioku iolu Newson Ra Summ ms es Wwright

Mughal
Jose Houdini, Fabio Florez

Mughal is a typeface that merges the timeless grace of blackletter with alluring oriental influences. Fueled by their fascination for hidden Oriental threads woven into contemporary typefaces, Fabio and Jose embarked on a quest to infuse this rich heritage into their creation. The font's elemental components beckon experimentation, transitioning from a personal exploration to a collaborative journey with Fabio. Seamlessly blending Jose's inventive spirit with Fabio's profound typeface design acumen, the combined efforts brought the typeface to life.

The name "Mughal" pays homage to a vibrant South Asian empire that flourished from 1526 to 1857, a nod to the empire's elegantly curved Khanjars—daggers that sparked the playful idea of envisioning the alphabet as a captivating Moghul army.

Classification
Neo Blackletter

Styles
N/A

Release
2019

Contact
josehoudini.es
@josehoudini.es
fabioflorez.com
@fabioflorez.design

NUGEN
NUGEN
NUGEN

TYPEFACE   BORN FROM
CONTEMPORARY REFERENCES AND
HISTORICAL
                  RESEARCH.

Mystica
Kevin Moll, Lena Manger

Originally being created as a custom font for the online platform "collide24," Mystica quickly turned from a few rough sketches into a collaborative long-term project between the two of us. Working together in a ping-pong-like manner, our different styles and ideas added up to a contemporary approach in type design—and to our first typeface ever.

      The idea was to create a typeface that would combine some characteristics of a Didone-like typeface with a modern, contemporary look. While the use of different widths of the strokes and the striking serifs reminds of old, ancient books, the extended width and the unusual shaping of the letters pursue a more futuristic approach. The clashing of those contrary characteristics leads not only to the name 'Mystica', but also to a dynamic and energetic look.

Classification
N/A

Styles
N/A

Release
2019

Contact
lenamanger.com
@lnmngr
kevinmoll.de
@kevin__moll

NAHEGLUT
Isabella Ramos Menzel

Since ancient Greece, the rose has been known as the Queen of Flowers. Its round shapes represent a radiant elegance while its thorns symbolize danger. These contrasts and its irresistible fragrance make it my favorite flower. The climbing rose NAHEGLUT is a very special breed. In 1997, the Danish breeder Poulsen introduced this flower, which serves as the basis of my typeface. NAHEGLUT is a rare and capricious type of rose that can reach heights up to three meters and flourishes in rich dark red. Its enormous height inspired the delicate lightcut, which refers to NAHEGLUT's elegance. The slant of my typeface derives from the image of roses moving in the wind—magnificent, proud, and intensive. Ralph Waldo Emerson, an American poet, once said, "Life is a journey, not a destination." My goal was never to construct a perfect typeface, but to learn as much as I could along the way. That's why NAHEGLUT is not finished yet and probably never will be, as it was just a wonderful experiment.

Classification
Modern Neoclassicist Antiqua

Styles
Light Oblique

Release
N/A

Contact
@bellaramee

merci pour

POULSEN
ROSE NAHEGLUT

pour

SECRET MESSAGE
AFFECTION
DEMONSTRATION   of   LOVE
EXPRESSION

GRATITUDE

TRUST

tout

AMOUR   ET   PASSION

TYPEFACE
NAHEGLUT LIGHT OBLIQUE   IRM

BEAUTY

Neustadt
Samara Keller

Neustadt#77F fuses the contemporary aesthetics of digital design with subtle hints of the gothic elegance found in blackletter typefaces. Applying a slight angle to the glyphs helps break the rigid nature of blackletter shapes and complements the sharp endings and spider-like extensions. This disharmonious convergence results in a font that embodies both tradition and modernity in an uncanny design.

With the essence of digital objects, mirroring the look of a calculator, and the opulence added by extravagant details, Neustadt#77F is a font that encapsulates the essence of forgetting your math homework at the rave. Neustadt#77F is only available in one style. The character set is in unicase and has a selected set of extended characters.

Classification
Gothic Calculator

Styles
77F

Release
2018

Contact
@keller_samara

CASTRO

NEU
STADT

#IFFA

Noodle
Mălin Neamțu (Apriko Type Foundry)

Noodle is inspired by street stories and Ramen. It includes one weight for now, categorized as "Ramen" as this would be the starting point for other weights such as "Udon" and "Tokoroten." The typeface started as research regarding letterform systems, shape expression, and language. Its inspiration came from vernacular typography throughout the city of Leipzig, eating Ramen during the night on the streets, and Pichação. Noodle's intended use is to explore its graphic possibilities and push the limits of letterform systems. It can be stretched, squished, inflated, deflated, or used as it comes out of the box—designer's choice. Essentially, its purpose is to contribute to fun posters, flyers, or identities.

Classification
Display

Styles
Ramen

Release
2018

Contact
@jesuismalin

Nostra
Lucas Descroix

Nostra plays with a feeling of satisfaction: how a few thin strokes can create the shape of a letter, either cut in a solid mass or traced in the air. Its monospaced width makes Nostra almost pattern-like, halfway between a legible and an abstract system, a block of text and an optical illusion.

Nostra presents an atypical couple only brought together by their radical proportions. The Sett is heavy and stable like a brick wall, while the Stream, inspired by flourished scripts, graffiti, and snakes in jars, is light and all in curves. Both styles cover Latin, Cyrillic, and Greek, as well as a selection of patterns and emojis.

Classification
Monospace Display

Styles
Sett
Stream

Release
2019

Contact
plain-form.com

Nova
Kai Udema

The design of Nova originated from a fascination with roundness in typography. The letter was drawn based on a simple grid but gained its characteristics from rounding all corners and white spaces. These white spaces are what make the letter most interesting. The round shapes shift one's focus to the white spaces more easily than with rectangular shapes and emphasize its cell-like appearance. The combination of a somewhat outdated method of grid-based drawing with a more contemporary organic aesthetic is what led to the name "Nova", suggesting a futuristic perspective while also referencing a retro idea of what we understand as futuristic.

Classification
N/A

Styles
Regular

Release
2019

Contact
kaiudema.com
@kaiudema

The shapes of its limbs are the products of a process related to its own survival. By the time its new limbs have grown into fully matured ones, in them small holes will start to appear. Over time, the holes will expand until they reach the outer edges of the surfaces, unifying with the voids of the world, like the collapsing of a dam that connects an isolated lake with the vast ocean. The process will continue until the right balance between a physical stability and a generous absence of matter in the limbs is reached.

Accordingly so it resides best in dark circumstances. Although it has no eyes to look with, in its perception this organism understands the world as overly bright, too bright really. From a Western perspective we tend to think of darkness as a visualization of the negative, the bad, and light as the positive. Though, this organism teaches us darkness is about sensitivity, rather than negativity. In a way darkness is no more than an absence of energy, as bright light is an overdue of energy, and this organism experiences the world more bright in darker places.

Supposedly, the function of the holes is to reduce the amount of light hitting it's surface. It tends to collect the needed amount of light to grow, but is equally sensitive to light, argumenting of physical dissolvement. Meaning, in a most paradoxical manner; it ought to dissolve as much as it can in order to stay alive, in order to remain.

It has limbs but no organs, as a matter of fact. Biologically this enables it to dissolve or grow in any direction it prefers to. This also gives it a somewhat fluid metabolism, and makes for a soft touch in comparison to other species. As its dissolvement allows to dose the amount of light it receives, this also enables it to reside in windy places, despite its lightweightedness that comes with it. Ever so magically, this again means that its retreatment out of the world, and into voids, grounds what's left of its presence in a fluid and passive strenght.

ODB
Tobias Holzmann

ODB is an experiment. It's an exercise, rather than a typeface. ODB is all about weight and contrast. Back in black and blacker than ever. Thins complement as hairlines. Upper- and lowercase letters are dramatically different from each other, yet they work well together. While the former has an almost archaic approach, the latter comes along with a more detailed appearance. The numbers encompass both directions.

ODB draws its inspiration from the famous Wu-Tang Clan logo, designed by Ronald Maurice Bean a.k.a. Mathematics, but also from more traditional typefaces like Bodoni or Caslon. It's axis is mostly inclined, but with room for exceptions.

ODB creates and uses its own rules. An outsider in the world of typography. A world where there is no right or wrong. Wu-Tang is for the children. ODB is for everyone.

Classification
High Contrast
Experimental
Sans Serif

Styles
Black

Release
2023

Contact
tobiasholzmann.com
@tobiasholzmann

Oskar
Robert Radziejewski

Oskar is a modular typeface consisting only of full, half, and quarter circle parts. Its geometric construction is not too rigid, incorporating illustrative moments that add a playful and less strict appearance. Each letter has an alternative shape, emphasizing its playful character. Oskar's various weights can be used in the classic way—from light to bold—but can also be set with the same stroke width and different cap-heights. This feature enables complex layouts with varying font sizes and consistent stroke widths. Overall, Oskar is inspired by the geometry of Bauhaus, infused with a touch of humor while adhering to its underlying rules.

Classification
Geometric Monolinear

Styles
Five Weights

Release
2017

Contact
radzie.de
@robert.radziejewski

OSKAR IS A GEOMET-
RIC TYPEFACE THAT
CONSISTS OF ONLY
TWO SIMPLE SHAPES.
IT STARTED AS A
TYPOGRAPHIC EXER-
CISE WHILE DRAWING
LETTERFORMS ON A
SHEET OF PAPER WITH
A SQUARED GRID AND

ENDED UP AS A TYPOGRAPHY
EXPERIMENT. EVERY GLYPH
IS BUILT OUT OF SQUARES
(FURTHER REFFERED AS PIXELS)
AND QUARTER-CIRCULAR
SHAPES THOSE ROUND SHAPES
VARY IN SIZE BUT REMAIN
AT THE SAME THICKNESS
OSKAR HAS FIVE DIFFERENT
CUTS. THE WEIGHT OF EACH

OUT IS DETERMINED BY THE PIXEL-
HEIGHT. IT SO HAPPENS THAT OS-
KARS APPROACH TOWARDS DIFFERENT
WEIGHTS IS NOT BY THICKNESS OF
THE STROKE BUT BY THE DISTANCE A
STROKE HAS TO TRAVEL FROM THE
BOTTOM TO THE TOP OF THE LET-
TER. THE INDIVIDUAL PIXEL-HEIGHTS
ARE 7, 10, 14, 18 AND 24 PIXELS. EACH
CUT COMES WITH ALTERNATIVE UPPER-

CASE LETTERS TO MAKE OSKAR EVEN MORE FUN AND
VERSATILE OSKAR IS CLEARLY ISPIRED BY THE SQUA-
RED GRID AND THE GEOMETRY AND SIMPLICITY OF THE
BAUHAUS WHICH IS ALSO WHERE THE NAME OSKAR
(SCHLEMMER) DERIVES FROM. OSKAR FEELS MOST
COMFORTABLE WHEN USED ON POSTERS, HEADLINES
OR OTHER APPLICATIONS THAT DO NOT NECESSARILY
REQUIRE THE BEST READABILITY BUT A MORE EXPRES-
SIVE STYLE. EVEN THOUGH OSKAR IS PRETTY LEGIBLE
AT ITS SMALLER PIXEL-HEIGHTS 7 AND 10. BUT ONCE

ONCE YOU SQUEEZE OSKAR AND MAKE ITS PHYSICAL HEIGHT THE SAME
WHILE USING DIFFERENT CUTS YOU GET DIFFERENT STROKE THICK-
NESSES AND A MORE CLASSIC FEEL OF A TYPEFACE WITH DIFFERENT
WEIGHTS.

Pala
Stefano Bona

Creating a typeface emerges by following an instinct. At least I like to believe that what I create originates somehow from unknown domains. And I enjoy evaluating the referential origins after I've finalized a project. It keeps me aware of how I perceive and react: When I look at Pala, I think about my background as a product designer. In the end, the focus lies on creating shapes that have certain optical stability. I see type design as a perpetual balance. Everything that throws off that balance becomes somehow obscure in its redundancy. I've never been interested in atemporal things, things that keep "up to date" through-out time. I don't really believe something like that exists. Pala is some-how current, perishable. Something that will probably become irrelevant in some time, but that's okay. I believe in upgrades. They keep me focused on the "now." I guess I'm more into that.

Classification
Display Extended

Styles
N/A

Release
2016

Contact
stefanobona.net
@stefanobonastefano

Planet Caravan
Kirill Ratman

Planet Caravan is a non-commercial experimental typeface with an enormously high stroke contrast. It has random sequence of horizontal and vertical line width and jumping stroke height for visual perception compensation. Having no rounded shapes at all Planet Caravan still has its vibe of semi-retro space mission and polygonally splashed into this mood.

I started to experiment with contrast, using only horizontals and vertical. No bends. Wanted the contrast level between the strokes to be as big as it could allow itself to be. In the end having the rhythm of these bolder elements behaving like you are staring at them with blurred vision.

Planet Caravan was awarded with the Type Directors Club Certificate of Typographic Excellence in 2019.

Classification
Experimental

Styles
Planet Caravan

Release
2019

Contact
@kiratman

PLASTICWELT
Javier Rodriguez

Manifestos on napkins, telephone numbers on skin, and accidents on the walls—PLASTICWELT feels at home in this kind of typography. It's a typeface trying to express feelings, personality, or a specific moment of the cultural graphic archive. A font aiming to represent a specific community, a font aiming to translate sound, a font aiming to dance!!

Classification
Display

Styles
N/A

Release
2019

Contact
@user00000017

[INTRO: Soto 454]
'Taba esperando a que llamaras
o a que vinieras
pa' sacarte fuera
y coger carretera

[ESTRIBILLO: Soto 454]
'Taba esperando a que llamaras
o a que vinieras
pa' sacarte fuera
y coger carretera

'Taba esperando a que llamaras
o a que vinieras
pa' sacarte fuera
y coger carretera

[VERSO : Soto 454]
Iba camino al infierno
en gráficas de Nintendo
dice que si compro, si vendo
esto no lo para ni un tremendo

Me gustaron sus nai (aí   aí)
Pone que no esta online (aí   aí)

Ponte las cortez y vente pa'aquí conmigo
Vamo' a hacerla bien ya no quiero enemigos
Puedes seguir viviendo retando al destino
Te espero con un escándalo distinto

[ESTRIBILLO: Soto 454]
'Taba esperando a que llamaras
o a que vinieras
pa' sacarte fuera
y coger carretera

Pluton
Benoît Canaud

Pluton reflects a symbiosis between editorial content, "fragments," and a variable and extreme font that gives it its identity. I started drawing the family in 2015 during my DNAT at ESAD Valence, just before the OpenType 1.8 format update. Initially inspired by a 1925 Bauer Foundry specimen and influenced by American sources, Pluton is emerging through a confrontation of heritage and modernity. It combines fixed elements with movement and adapts to reading situations in both text and display, as well as in print and screen applications. I was intrigued by the metamorphosis of text and how it transforms through technical interpolation. Just like the formats, the rendering of the letters evolves on screen and a new adaptive optical scale becomes reality.

Classification
Grotesk

Styles
Condensed
Middle
Extended

Release
2017

Contact
focaltype.com
@focal.type
@benoitcanaud

Polyphem
Tobias Hönow

The first version of Polyphem was drawn back in 2017 for the identity of the conference "Micky loves Polyphem." The conference dealt with the virtual image of humans in digital spaces. In addition to the original Monospace, which was a gruffy homage to the iconic OCR-A from 1968, a Regular and an Italic style were added in 2023, expanding the typeface to a fully variable family. Polyphem is a modularly constructed typeface which is based on a 45° grid. With its sharp edges and clean forms, Polyphem works perfectly well in small body text sizes but also in large headline sizes—in analog as well as in digital applications.

Classification
Linear Geometric

Styles
Regular
Italic
Mono

Release
2017, 2023

Contact
tobiashoenow.de
@tobiashoenow

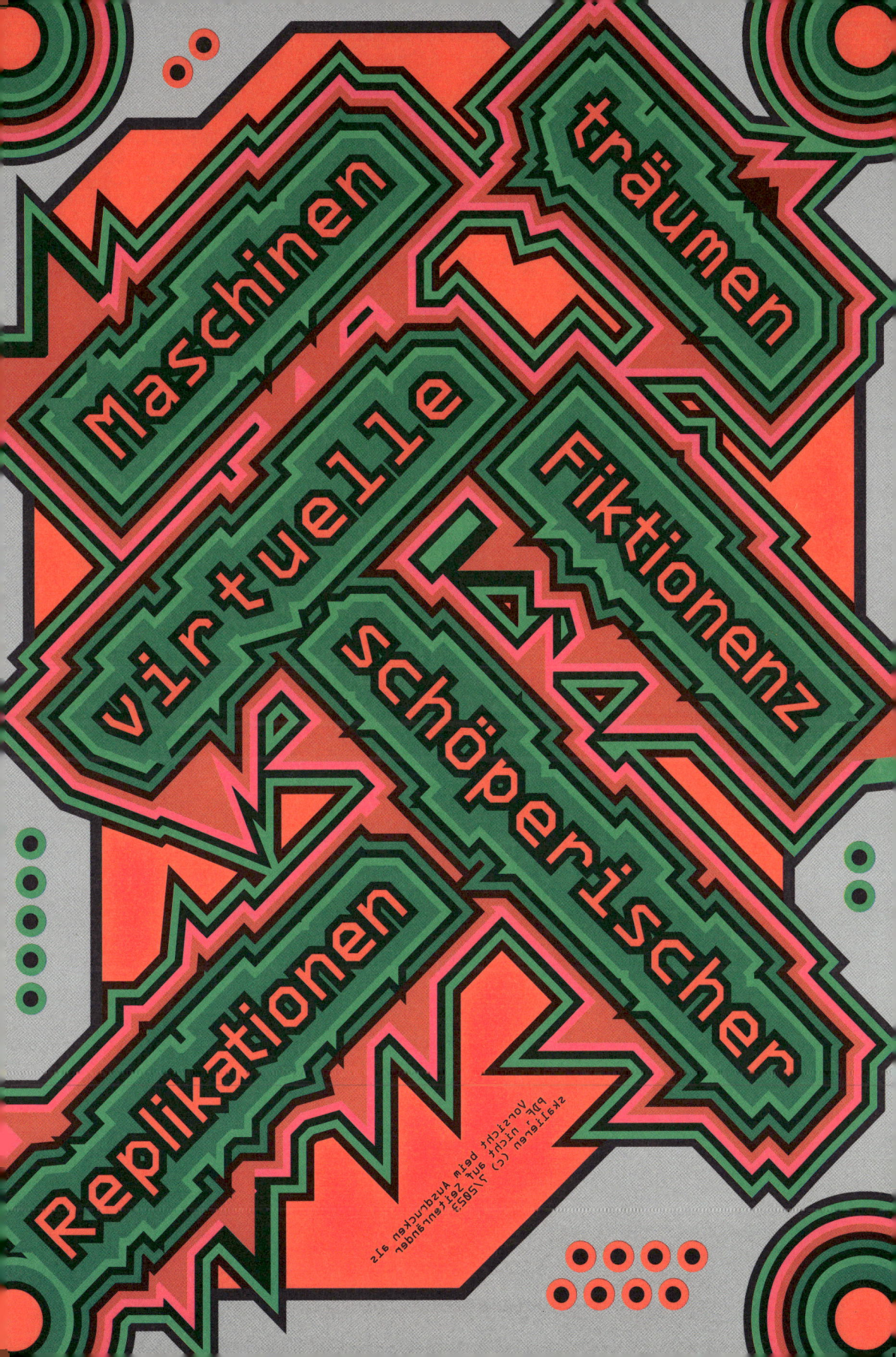

Maschinen träumen virtuelle Fiktionenz schöperischer Replikationen

Portico
Laura Hilbert

Portico is a very flexible modular typeface that comes in a big variety of styles. It is made of the negative space of squares, circles, semi-circles, and triangles, which are placed at the corners of any chosen format. The negative space created by this pattern helps to form a lot of different glyphs. Portico works best when printed in very large sizes and especially when shown in movement since it is very adaptable and likes to transform. The range of widths, weights, and x-heights can even be extended because it is a variable font.

Classification
Display

Styles
Regular	**Bold**
Semi Condesed	**Black**
Condensed	**Medium X-Height**
Extended	**Small X-Height**
Ultra Extended	

Release
2018

Contact
laurahilbert.de
@laura_hilbert

abcdefghijklmnopqrstuvwxyzabcdefghijklmnopqrstuvwxyzabcdefghij
klmnopqrstuvwxyzabcdefghijklmnopqr
stuvwxyzabcdefghijklmno
pqrstuvwxyzabcdef
ghijklmnopqrst
uvwxyzabcd
efghijklm
hopqrst
uvwxyz

rrrpppppp

portico typeface

Repro
Erkin Karamemet (Dinamo)

Repro is a friendly, flexible sans-serif inspired by signage and digital operating systems; it's a typeface that merges clean design with complex font engineering.

The extensive family includes nine weights with italics, as well as a monospaced variant and a variety of OpenType features, forming a comprehensive toolkit for users developing experiences both online or offline. As a customizable Variable Font, Repro is open-ended, with system functionality and digital interfaces in mind.

In addition to its range of sharp or soft alternates, the typeface contains a unique tool for circled emphasis, offering users a beautiful new way to create visual hierarchy. And while Repro has an overall geometric feel, it's softer and more personable than the mechanical typefaces it shares a community garden with. It's design is bold, reliable, and recognizable, with a range of alternatives, web-specific glyphs, and more, which can be mix-and-matched to create a variety of different rhythms and flavors.

Classification
Sans Serif

Styles
72 Weights

Release
2019

Contact
erkinkaramemet.com
@erkin_karamemet

EXIT A1-29

ARRIVAL

200m

Train Stations

TERMINAL

↓ Infopoint

EXIT

Terminals

B2 ↑

Baggage Claim

Ribasuu
Tien-Min Liao

In a reverse-contrast typeface, the normal weight distribution is reversed. The result is that the weight becomes concentrated along the cap-height, x-height, and baseline, creating a strong horizontal visual connection. Unlike the Latin alphabet, the weight distribution in Kanji and Kana is much more complex, and the weight is not just on the verticals. Many strokes are diagonal or curved, so the weight distribution varies on different strokes. Simply reversing the weight distribution may not create the same visual result as in the Latin one. Instead of reversing the weight literally, my approach is to create a typeface that captures the visual essence of the Latin reverse-contrast. That essence is the quirky personality and strong horizontal connection; therefore, both can work together in a visually compatible way.

Classification
Reverse Contrast

Styles
N/A

Release
N/A

Contact
typeji.com

Latin, カナ＆漢字 東京

Latin   Hiragana and Katakana   Kanji

Rygor
Maciej Połczyński

Rygor is based on a book cover of "Plays and games as a factor in upbringing" by Stanisław Karpowicz, published in Warsaw in 1910. Both the lettering and the illustration seemed very crude—presenting an eagle in the nest on the red background, facing his nestlings. Most probably the lettering was created by Ignacy Chodorowicz—illustrator and publisher of that period.

The typeface is built out of 9 characters that appear in the title (Wychowanie—Upbringing) and it is a typical approach of early 20th century style—unequal proportions of both the middle bars and the shapes themselves. Various letters are possible in alternative forms to create a more common look. The way a stem is connected to a serif might seem harsh or rigorous—as the name of the typeface.

Rygor was extended to consist of Cyrillic and Greek scripts along with Latin (859 glyphs in total).

Classification
Display

Styles
N/A

Release
2018

Contact
@LaicType

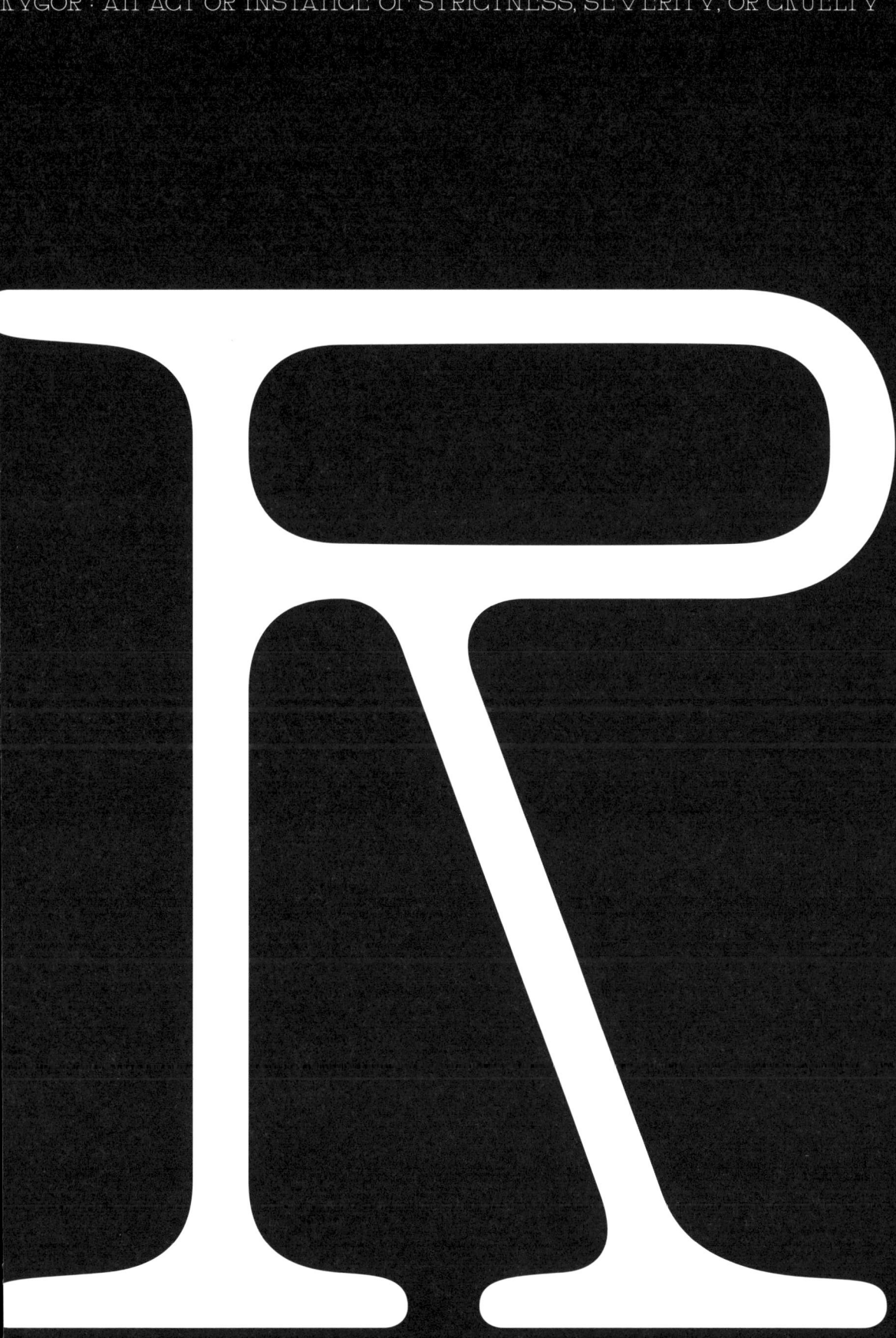

Serpe
Raphaël de La Morinerie

Serpe is a contemporary serif typeface with a timeless charm, offering a range of six distinct styles, spanning from Thin to Black. As the weight increases, so does the character's contrast. The thinner styles gracefully suit body text, while the bolder ones elegantly command attention on impactful messages. Infused with the essence of lapidary typography and accentuated by its asymmetrical serif, reminiscent of calligraphic strokes, Serpe's drawing exudes a unique appeal. Drawing inspiration from the depths of typographic history, Serpe also emits a minimalist allure that embraces a digital flare.

The design journey of Serpe began in 2018 and is currently undergoing an entire revision. Its new version is set to be released in 2023 at WrittenShape Type Foundry, promising a revitalized and enhanced typographic gem.

Classification
Display
Serif

Styles
Thin	**Black**
Light	
Regular	
Medium	
Bold	

Release
2023

Contact
writtenshape.com
@writtenshape

aaaaaabbbbbbcccccc ddddd gggggg kkkkkk qqqqqq
eeeeee hhhhhh llllll rrrrrr
ffffff iiiiii mmmmmm ssssss
jjjjjj nnnnnn tttttt
oooooo uuuuuu
pppppp vvvvvv
wwwww
xxxxxx
yyyyyy
zzzzzzZ

FLIP THE COIN AND LET FATE SHOW ITS HAND

Shrill
PizzaTypefaces

The Shrill typeface explores the limit of inverted contrast in type design. It renders a cowboy-style font feeling in bolder weight but can offer a different feel depending on the size. Playing with weight distribution and long serifs, the design simultaneously provides an aggressive, twisted, monospaced, and soft flavor. In large size, Shrill gives an impression of aggressiveness with its serifs really "sharked." In small size, it becomes like a typewriter font. Shrill is supporting Cyrillic script. Variable and static font with 2 axes, and a full OTF font family with 7 weights and italics ranging from Thin to Black supporting Latin, Latin Plus & Cyrillic languages. MoreScript™!

Classification
Spaghetti Movie
Invert
Sans Serif

Styles
Variable Font

Release
2020

Contact
typefaces.pizza

Shrill Latin + Cyrillic

Shrill typeface is a variable font in weight exploring the limit of inverted contrast in type design.

Siluett
Andree Paat (Tüpokompanii)

Siluett is a display typeface that plays on the boundaries of traditional type design conventions. Looking at the features of various typefaces in the Modern classification, Siluett aims to go further by pushing the limits of elegance and expressiveness, balancing on the edge of good and bad taste. Serifs are elongated to the point of being almost unbearable, weights range from the delicate Thin to the massive Ultra, italics sprint at an extreme 25 degree angle, rounded forms are emphasized by an inner vacuum-like tension, and so on. Although taking cues from the past, Siluett is firmly positioned in the contemporary type design landscape with its inherently digital drawing qualities and surgically precise details.

Classification
Modern
Display
Serif

Styles
Thin to Ultra
Italics

Release
N/A

Contact
typokompanii.com
@typokompanii

Here's What It Would Look Like If You *Guccified* Your Home

Headline from AnOther Magazine, 2019

Sketleton
Fabian Maier-Bode

The typeface design was part of fraser muggeridge's typography summer school in 2016. The task was to create a unique take on an existing analog phototypesetting typeface. Sketleton is based on a simple line-like skeleton, which is the basis for exporting font styles through different boldings. In addition to the missing glyphs of the reference, new design choices have been made primarily in serifs, angles, and kerning, as well as alternative glyphs as stylistic sets. The reinterpretation of the original phototype setting is designed to create vintage 90's UK rave flyers. Using different degrees of saturation, distortion or other transformations, Sketleton offers many different ways to interpret the vibrant excesses of this scene and time in a visually exciting way.

Classification
**Digital Revival of a
Phototypesetting Font**

Styles
**Light
Regular
Bold**

Release
2017

Contact
**fabianmaierbode.de
@fabianamaierbode**

Solid
Alessio D'Ellena

Solid is a strong, compact and blocky typeface primarily intended for display use, typographic logos and compositions. The counters are rational basic circles, and this feature is corrupted by the outer extra-squared contours, creating a dialogue between inner and outer squareness. Drawn down on brutalist design principles and a pure sense of balance, Solid is a "ready to wear" typeface. The letter shapes are simplified and pushed to the extreme, winking to the basic Euclidean geometry. Compact, thick and extra bold, for now, but yet ready to be expanded into a more linear type family through the weight axis.

Classification
Display

Styles
Fat
Extra Bold

Release
Unpublished

Contact
@alessio_dellena

ard, Bri
ck.
→ Con
crete: dull
or strong
Solid.

Spirella
Jules Durand

A take on two classic types from the letterpress era; Cabinet, designed by Ernst Lauschke in 1888, patented and assigned to Barnhart Brothers & Spindler, and Spiral, designed by Herman Ihlenburg in 1890, distributed by MacKellar, Smith & Jordan. These faces demonstrate a feeling of psychedelia, mysticism, and fantasy with their unique spirals and blooming scrolls. A lack of reliable revivals for both of them leads me to consider doing a mashup, on the basis of a stroke font, to easily extend the line from Thin to Bold. The typeface includes quirky alternates with more spirals, as well as a set of stormy letters like sxkCRQTX39 and a bunch of non-standard ligatures and symbols. Lastly, a set of inclusive ligatures is being developed (to be properly encoded) along with inclusive diacritics below the letters.

Classification
Display

Styles
Regular
Bold

Release
2023

Contact
julesdurand.com
@lazy_dog.ttf

The Sails are Set, the Magestic Frigate Night

∴ And Spires seem Moving to the Left ∴

∻ 12845 & 64890 ∻

The Narthex is a place of transition

between the outside & the inside,

the profane and the sacred.

Devastating EarthQuakes

after Sauron fall in Mordor

The Forgotten

REALM

Streetfutura
Sascha Bente

Streetfutura is on the one hand a humorous homage to the classic New York graffiti aesthetic of the 1970s—but on the other hand it is also a reference to geometrically constructed poster fonts. It was drawn by hand and transferred to the type software without corrections, so that inconsistencies and inaccuracies are accepted rather than excluded. The surface of the typeface is significantly influenced by the felt-tip pen, creating small imperfections that make it appear vibrant. Streetfutura appears as an uppercase-only single cut typeface and was created during Master Type Design at ECAL in 2019.

Classification
Display

Styles
Poster

Release
2019

Contact
saschabente.com
@sascha.bente

NEW YORK
LAUSANNE
(WEIMAR) ECAL

ROLAND TR808
BREAKBEAT
DAS BAUHAUS
BRONX 1312
HELVETICA (NOW)
ZÜRICH 1973

1919
1987

ABCDEFGHIJKLMN
OPQRSTUWXYZ
12345678
90.,;:?()

MAN PARRISH
ELECTRO CITY
4 TO THE FLOOR
PROFESSOR X
MIAMI SUB BASS
DYNAMIX 909
EGYPTIAN LOVER

STREETFUTURA

Sveta
Aimur Takk (Tüpokompanii)

Sveta Bold Condensed Display was developed within AKU Collective for Tallinn Music Week 2018 as its central branding device. With the focus on space-saving and a unique visual aesthetic for large display usage, it combines thin horizontal forms with contrasting verticals. The Cyrillic alphabet and various diacritical symbols and glyphs are included. "But why is its name Sveta?" you may ask. The name derives from when I started drawing the typeface at Sveta Bar in Tallinn during one great party event.

Classification
Mixed Contrast Grotesk

Styles
Sveta Bold Condensed Display
Sveta Bold Condensed Stencil

Release
2018

Contact
typokompanii.com
@typokompanii

Sveta
Bold
Condensed
Display

Света
Жирная
Сжатая
Заглавная

Graphic & Type Design
by Aimur Takk 2019

SWORD
Kazuhiro Aihara

SWORD was inspired by the way of how the Japanese samurai are moving their swords. The lines of the typeface resemble the curves and lines of how the Japanese sword slices through the air. I visualized the name of Beatrix Michelle Kiddo in my typographic poster to pay homage to Quentin Tarantino's well-known movie. The SWORD typeface is a visualized and also conceptualized typographical experimentation which flows out between legible and illegible.

Classification
Display

Styles
Regular

Release
2018

Contact
@kazuhiro_aihara

Taters
Tommi Sharp

Taters was developed during my time at Type@Cooper West as my original typeface design for the program. Its development was driven by an experimental drawing technique involving potatoes carved as stamps using a linoleum tool. This playful process allowed me to work very loosely and explore letter shapes from the inside out, which was liberating. The most significant challenge was wrangling the organic, unrestrained letterforms into a functional system. To prevent waste (and save my hands), I adopted a different iteration method—drawing with correction fluid on black paper to simulate carving the negative space around forms. Through a back-and-forth process of drawing and digitizing, I established a system of repeated shapes with a level of variation, preserving the essence of the original experiments. Special thanks to my teachers James Edmondson, Tânia Raposo, and Frank Grießhammer, as well as Cyrus Highsmith, whose negative space drawings inspired me.

Classification
Experimental

Styles
Baked
Mashed
Fried

Release
2019

Contact
tommisharp.com
@tommisharp

Taters

Served up in delicious 3 styles:

Baked Mashed & Fried

Taters Baked is an all-natural display typeface with no added colors, flavors, or sugar.

"Taters Fried is great for satisfying those late night cravings for a font designed with small sizes in mind. It looks great even at 8pt!"

"Taters is rooted in potato carvings. After an experimental drawing workshop at Type@Cooper West, I was inspired to whittle a gigantic potato I had into stamps and the initial seeds for Taters was planted."

Feast your eyes on Taters Mashed.

It's best served at 72pt (or larger) in a setting of 1-2 words that make up the main course. How would I sum up this style of Taters in just one word? Scrumptious!

Taters was carved by Tommi Sharp while attending Type@Cooper West in 2018. It's available at www.futurefonts.xyz

Urushi
Calvin Kwok

Urushi finds its roots in a personalized movie title I created for the "Havana Divas" documentary. This design brings to mind the charm of old Hong Kong movie magazines, capturing a certain nostalgic essence. Beyond this, Urushi is also influenced by the Flat Brush script calligraphy, which gained prominence during the Qing Dynasty, thanks to visionaries like Jin Nong. The font has a dynamic feel to it, combining reverse contrast and a dash of boldness that catches the eye. Urushi is both a nod to its historical inspiration and a testament to calligraphy's enduring appeal. Crafted to shine in displays and be effective in shorter texts, Urushi bridges the past and the present gracefully.

Classification
Reverse Contrast Slab Serif

Styles
N/A

Release
N/A

Contact
@calvinkwok.co

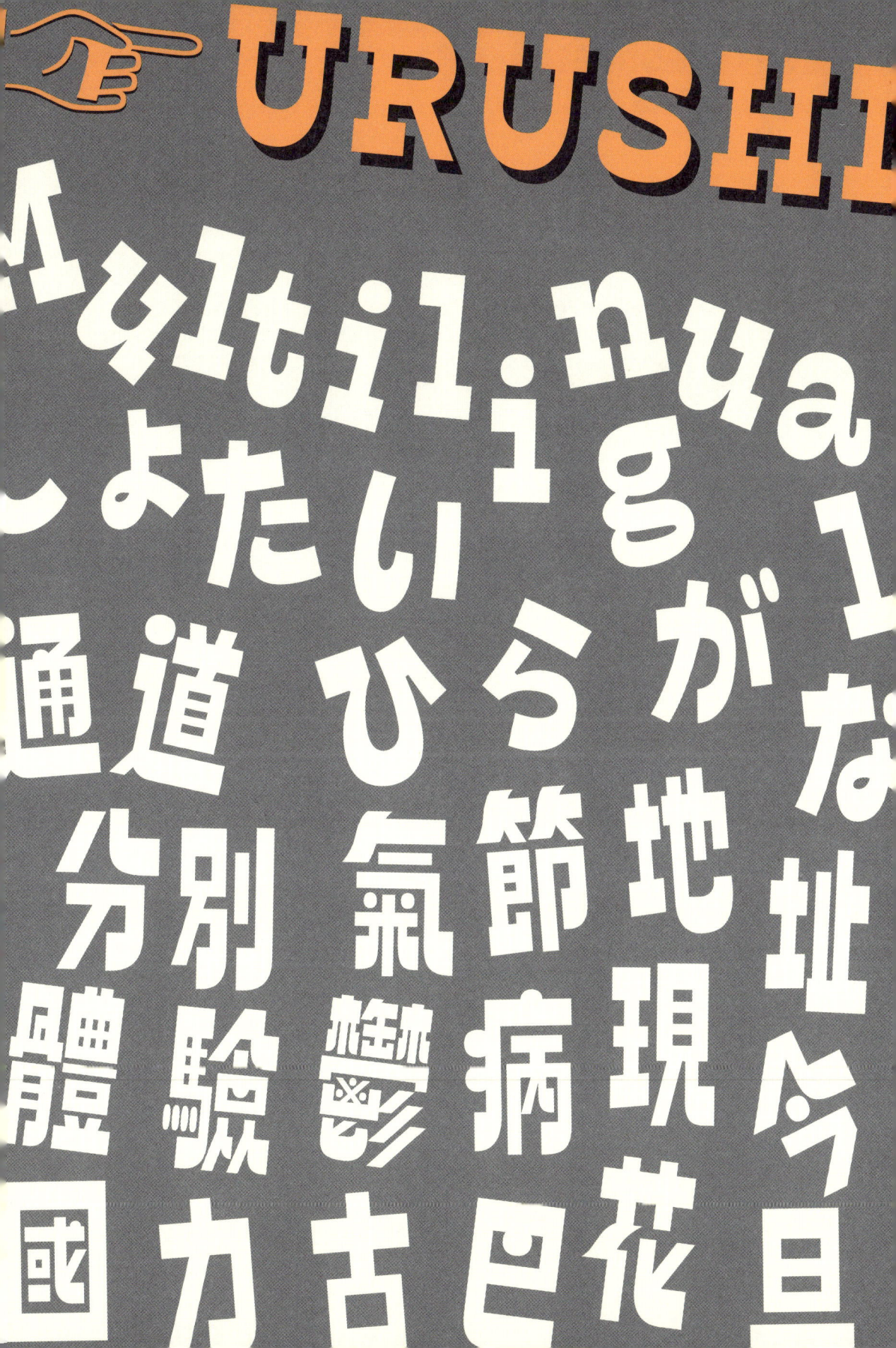

VZWO Elephant
Viktor Zumegen

VZWO Elephant is designed by Viktor Zumegen. It is a heavyset display font with high contrast, high x-height and an extremely compact effect. The result is a closed typeface with strongly accentuated verticals, created by the narrow width and thickness of the typeface. The individual letters fill the available space with a maximum of color. The typeface is dominated by highly waisted letters, deep inktraps, completely rounded shapes, tapers in the trunks and concave ends. VZWO Elephant has an organic character, it is strong and compact and yet knows how to retain a certain touch of elegance.

Classification
Display

Styles
Black

Release
2019

Contact
viktorzumegen.de
@viktorzumegen

Elephant

TYPEFACE BY VIKTOR ZUMEGEN

Zangezi
Daria Cohen

The Zangezi type family started as a revival of the single-style typeface Salem, discovered in a 1901 specimen by the Keystone Type Foundry. It is a work in progress (currently version 0.6) that distills the most exciting features of the original typeface and gradually sets off on its own. Strong color, sharp terminals, and an eccentric italic give Zangezi a brutal yet elegant appearance, where "yet" does not imply a compromise. Its serpentine, schizophrenic, ever-changing shapes are an expression of the pure joy of drawing. The type family currently consists of 6 styles and is most likely growing while you read this.

Classification
Display

Styles
Zangezi Regular   **Italic**
Semilight
Light
Italic
Zangezi Sans Regular

Release
2018 - 2019

Contact
dariapetrova.com
@typodaria

Zangezi*
light
semilight
regular
italic
Zangezi
Sans*
regular
italic
black

Zorn
Laura Csocsán

Zorn derives its essence from the dynamic directions of lowercase letters. All of the shapes are extended and quite light with noticeable contrast. There is as much tension inside one letter as possible, and also between different letters and numbers. It has an overall look of sudden, somewhat harsh movements conveyed by sharp forms. To maintain this tension and energy, not all contrasts adhere to the pen's natural style, which led to several questions and a path towards the most cohesive appearance but also the most intriguing shapes. While some concepts were initially sketched with a parallel pen on paper, certain ideas only emerged digitally with the letter's digitization.

Classification
Experimental

Styles
Regular

Release
2019

Contact
lauracsocsan.com
@cs__laura

12:15
Colin Doerffler

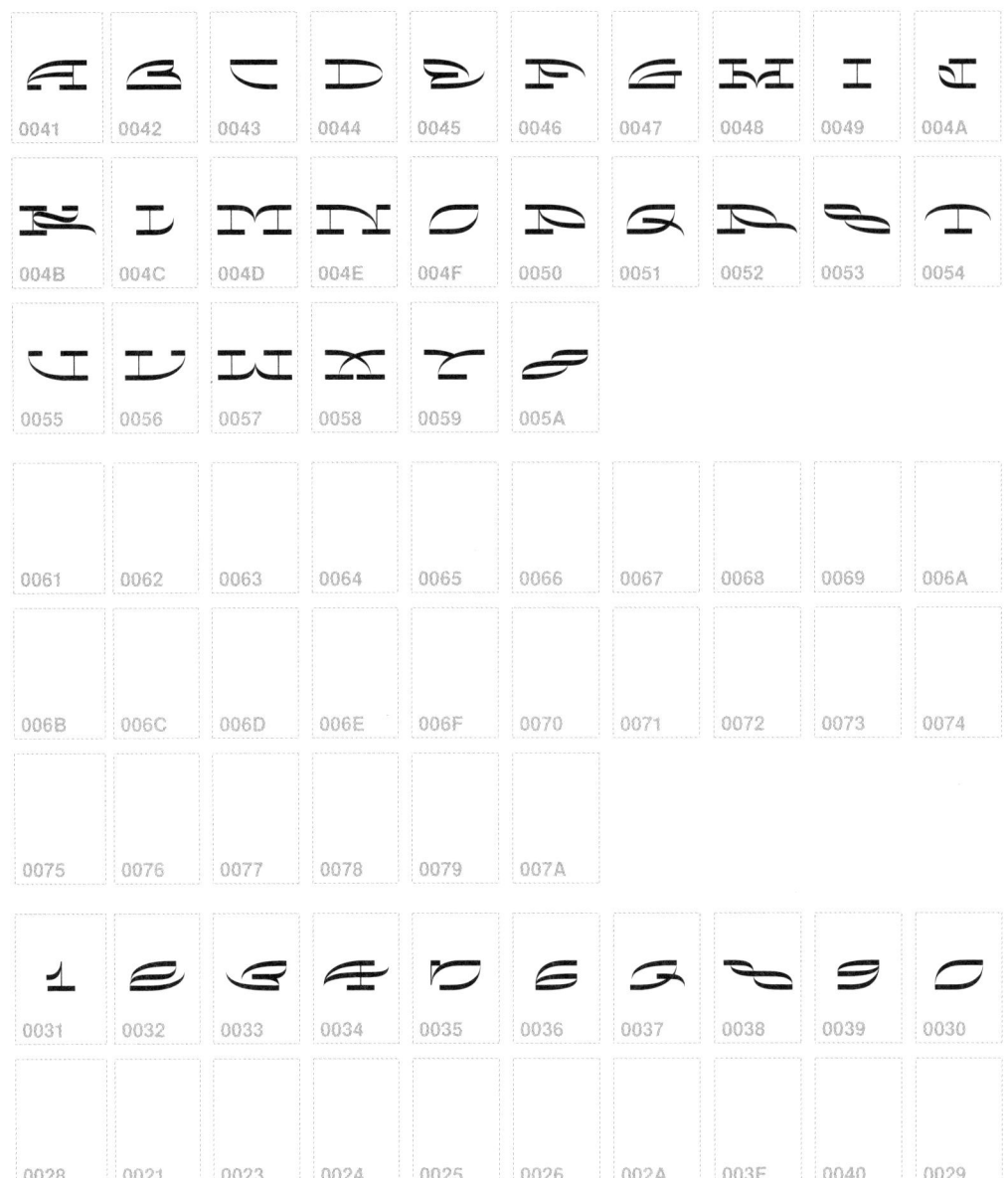

0041	0042	0043	0044	0045	0046	0047	0048	0049	004A
004B	004C	004D	004E	004F	0050	0051	0052	0053	0054
0055	0056	0057	0058	0059	005A				
0061	0062	0063	0064	0065	0066	0067	0068	0069	006A
006B	006C	006D	006E	006F	0070	0071	0072	0073	0074
0075	0076	0077	0078	0079	007A				
0031	0032	0033	0034	0035	0036	0037	0038	0039	0030
0028	0021	0023	0024	0025	0026	002A	003F	0040	0029

Aegi
Christian Horrer, Mario Naegele

A	B	C	D	E	F	G	H	I	J
0041	0042	0043	0044	0045	0046	0047	0048	0049	004A
K	L	M	N	O	P	Q	R	S	T
004B	004C	004D	004E	004F	0050	0051	0052	0053	0054
U	V	W	X	Y	Z				
0055	0056	0057	0058	0059	005A				

a	b	c	d	e	f	g	h	i	j
0061	0062	0063	0064	0065	0066	0067	0068	0069	006A
k	l	m	n	o	p	q	r	s	t
006B	006C	006D	006E	006F	0070	0071	0072	0073	0074
u	v	w	x	y	z				
0075	0076	0077	0078	0079	007A				

1	2	3	4	5	6	7	8	9	0
0031	0032	0033	0034	0035	0036	0037	0038	0039	0030
(	!	#	$	%	&	*	?	@	)
0028	0021	0023	0024	0025	0026	002A	003F	0040	0029

Airdancer
Massimiliano Audretsch, Moritz Appich, Bruno Jacoby (Gruppo Due)

A	B	C	D	E	F	G	H	I	J
0041	0042	0043	0044	0045	0046	0047	0048	0049	004A
K	L	M	N	O	P	Q	R	S	T
004B	004C	004D	004E	004F	0050	0051	0052	0053	0054
U	V	W	X	Y	Z				
0055	0056	0057	0058	0059	005A				
a	b	c	d	e	f	g	h	i	j
0061	0062	0063	0064	0065	0066	0067	0068	0069	006A
k	l	m	n	o	p	q	r	s	t
006B	006C	006D	006E	006F	0070	0071	0072	0073	0074
u	v	w	x	y	z				
0075	0076	0077	0078	0079	007A				
1	2	3	4	5	6	7	8	9	0
0031	0032	0033	0034	0035	0036	0037	0038	0039	0030
(	!						?		)
0028	0021	0023	0024	0025	0026	002A	003F	0040	0029

ALBINO
Lukas Manuel Altmann

𝔄	𝔅	ℭ	𝔇	𝔈	𝔉	𝔊	𝔥	𝕴	𝕵
0041	0042	0043	0044	0045	0046	0047	0048	0049	004A
𝔎	𝔏	𝔐	𝔑	𝔒	𝔓	𝔔	𝔕	𝔖	𝔗
004B	004C	004D	004E	004F	0050	0051	0052	0053	0054
𝔘	𝔙	𝔚	𝔛	𝔜	𝔝				
0055	0056	0057	0058	0059	005A				
a	b	c	d	e	f	g	h	i	j
0061	0062	0063	0064	0065	0066	0067	0068	0069	006A
k	l	m	n	o	p	q	r	s	t
006B	006C	006D	006E	006F	0070	0071	0072	0073	0074
u	v	w	x	y	z				
0075	0076	0077	0078	0079	007A				
0031	0032	0033	0034	0035	0036	0037	0038	0039	0030
0028	0021	0023	0024	0025	0026	002A	003F	0040	0029

APK Galeria
Peter Korsman (Autograph)

A	B	C	D	E	F	G	H	I	J
0041	0042	0043	0044	0045	0046	0047	0048	0049	004A
K	L	M	N	O	P	Q	R	S	T
004B	004C	004D	004E	004F	0050	0051	0052	0053	0054
U	V	W	X	Y	Z				
0055	0056	0057	0058	0059	005A				
a	b	c	d	e	f	g	h	i	j
0061	0062	0063	0064	0065	0066	0067	0068	0069	006A
k	l	m	n	o	p	q	r	s	t
006B	006C	006D	006E	006F	0070	0071	0072	0073	0074
u	v	w	x	y	z				
0075	0076	0077	0078	0079	007A				
1	2	3	4	5	6	7	8	9	0
0031	0032	0033	0034	0035	0036	0037	0038	0039	0030
(	!	#	§	%	&	*	?	@	)
0028	0021	0023	0024	0025	0026	002A	003F	0040	0029

Apparat
Michael Clasen, Marcel Saidov (kimera)

A	B	C	D	E	F	G	H	I	J
0041	0042	0043	0044	0045	0046	0047	0048	0049	004A
K	L	M	N	O	P	Q	R	S	T
004B	004C	004D	004E	004F	0050	0051	0052	0053	0054
U	V	W	X	Y	Z				
0055	0056	0057	0058	0059	005A				
a	b	c	d	e	f	g	h	i	j
0061	0062	0063	0064	0065	0066	0067	0068	0069	006A
k	l	m	n	o	p	q	r	s	t
006B	006C	006D	006E	006F	0070	0071	0072	0073	0074
u	v	w	x	y	z				
0075	0076	0077	0078	0079	007A				
1	2	3	4	5	6	7	8	9	0
0031	0032	0033	0034	0035	0036	0037	0038	0039	0030
(	!	#	§	%	&	*	?	@	)
0028	0021	0023	0024	0025	0026	002A	003F	0040	0029

Arachne
Leonhard Laupichler

A	B	C	D	E	F	G	H	I	J
0041	0042	0043	0044	0045	0046	0047	0048	0049	004A
K	L	M	N	O	P	Q	R	S	T
004B	004C	004D	004E	004F	0050	0051	0052	0053	0054
U	V	W	X	Y	Z				
0055	0056	0057	0058	0059	005A				
a	b	c	d	e	f	g	h	i	j
0061	0062	0063	0064	0065	0066	0067	0068	0069	006A
k	l	m	n	o	p	q	r	s	t
006B	006C	006D	006E	006F	0070	0071	0072	0073	0074
u	v	w	x	y	z				
0075	0076	0077	0078	0079	007A				
1	2	3	4	5	6	7	8	9	0
0031	0032	0033	0034	0035	0036	0037	0038	0039	0030
(	!	#			&	*	?	@	)
0028	0021	0023	0024	0025	0026	002A	003F	0040	0029

Architype 45 / 90
Sascha Bente

A	B	C	D	E	F	G	H	I	J
0041	0042	0043	0044	0045	0046	0047	0048	0049	004A
K	L	M	N	O	P	Q	R	S	T
004B	004C	004D	004E	004F	0050	0051	0052	0053	0054
U	V	W	X	Y	Z				
0055	0056	0057	0058	0059	005A				

0061	0062	0063	0064	0065	0066	0067	0068	0069	006A
006B	006C	006D	006E	006F	0070	0071	0072	0073	0074
0075	0076	0077	0078	0079	007A				

1	2	3	4	5	6	7	8	9	0
0031	0032	0033	0034	0035	0036	0037	0038	0039	0030
					&.				
0028	0021	0023	0024	0025	0026	002A	003F	0040	0029

Atlanta
Basile Fournier

A	B	C	D	E	F	G	H	I	J
0041	0042	0043	0044	0045	0046	0047	0048	0049	004A
K	L	M	N	O	P	Q	R	S	T
004B	004C	004D	004E	004F	0050	0051	0052	0053	0054
U	V	W	X	Y	Z				
0055	0056	0057	0058	0059	005A				
a	b	c	d	e	f	g	h	i	j
0061	0062	0063	0064	0065	0066	0067	0068	0069	006A
k	l	m	n	o	p	q	r	s	t
006B	006C	006D	006E	006F	0070	0071	0072	0073	0074
u	v	w	x	y	z				
0075	0076	0077	0078	0079	007A				
1	2	3	4	5	6	7	8	9	0
0031	0032	0033	0034	0035	0036	0037	0038	0039	0030
(	!	#	§	%	&	*	?	@	)
0028	0021	0023	0024	0025	0026	002A	003F	0040	0029

AURAE
Janik Sandbothe

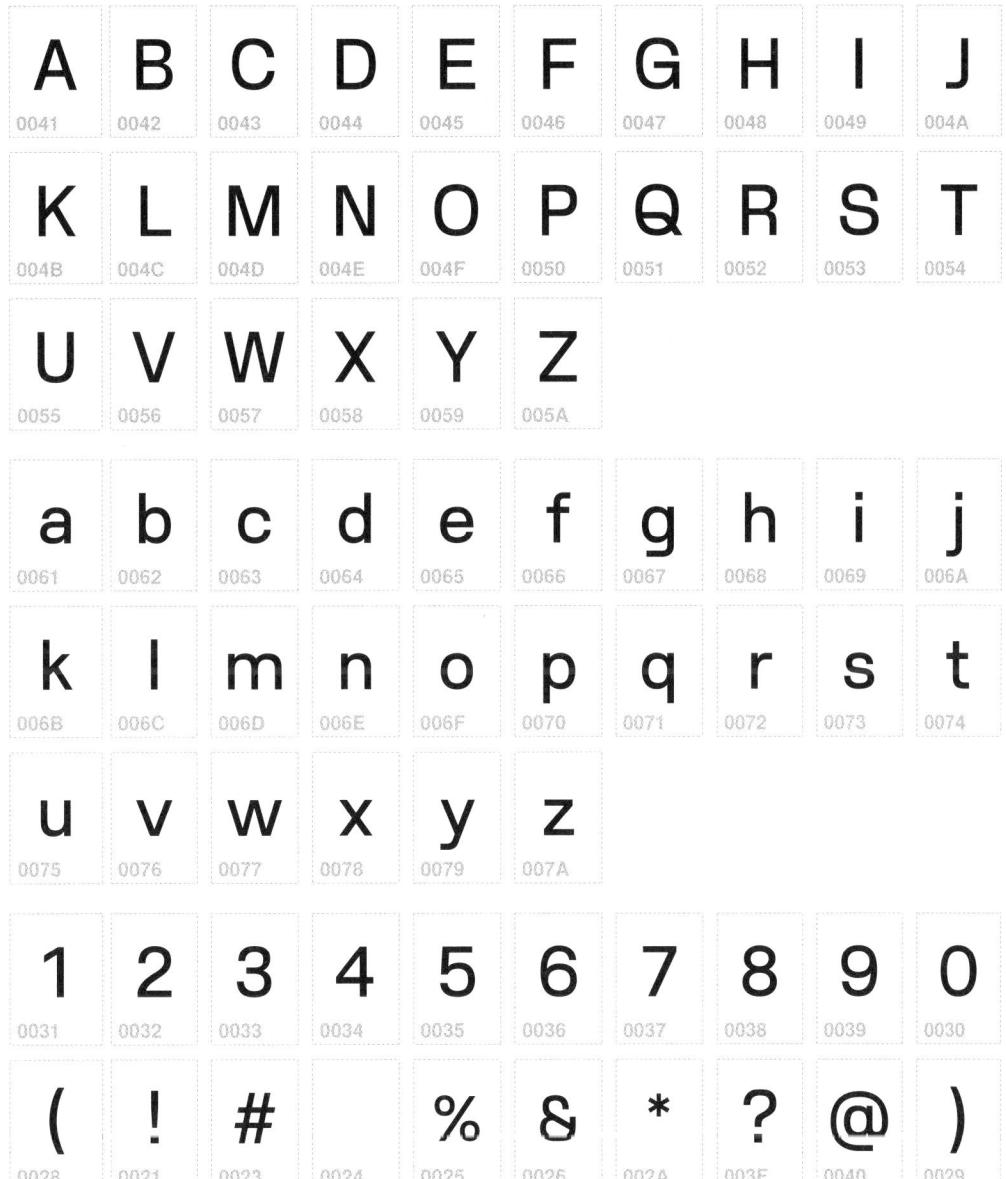

A 0041 B 0042 C 0043 D 0044 E 0045 F 0046 G 0047 H 0048 I 0049 J 004A

K 004B L 004C M 004D N 004E O 004F P 0050 Q 0051 R 0052 S 0053 T 0054

U 0055 V 0056 W 0057 X 0058 Y 0059 Z 005A

a 0061 b 0062 c 0063 d 0064 e 0065 f 0066 g 0067 h 0068 i 0069 j 006A

k 006B l 006C m 006D n 006E o 006F p 0070 q 0071 r 0072 s 0073 t 0074

u 0075 v 0076 w 0077 x 0078 y 0079 z 007A

1 0031 2 0032 3 0033 4 0034 5 0035 6 0036 7 0037 8 0038 9 0039 0 0030

(0028 ! 0021 # 0023 $ 0024 % 0025 & 0026 * 002A ? 003F @ 0040) 0029

Bad Mono
Tor Weibull

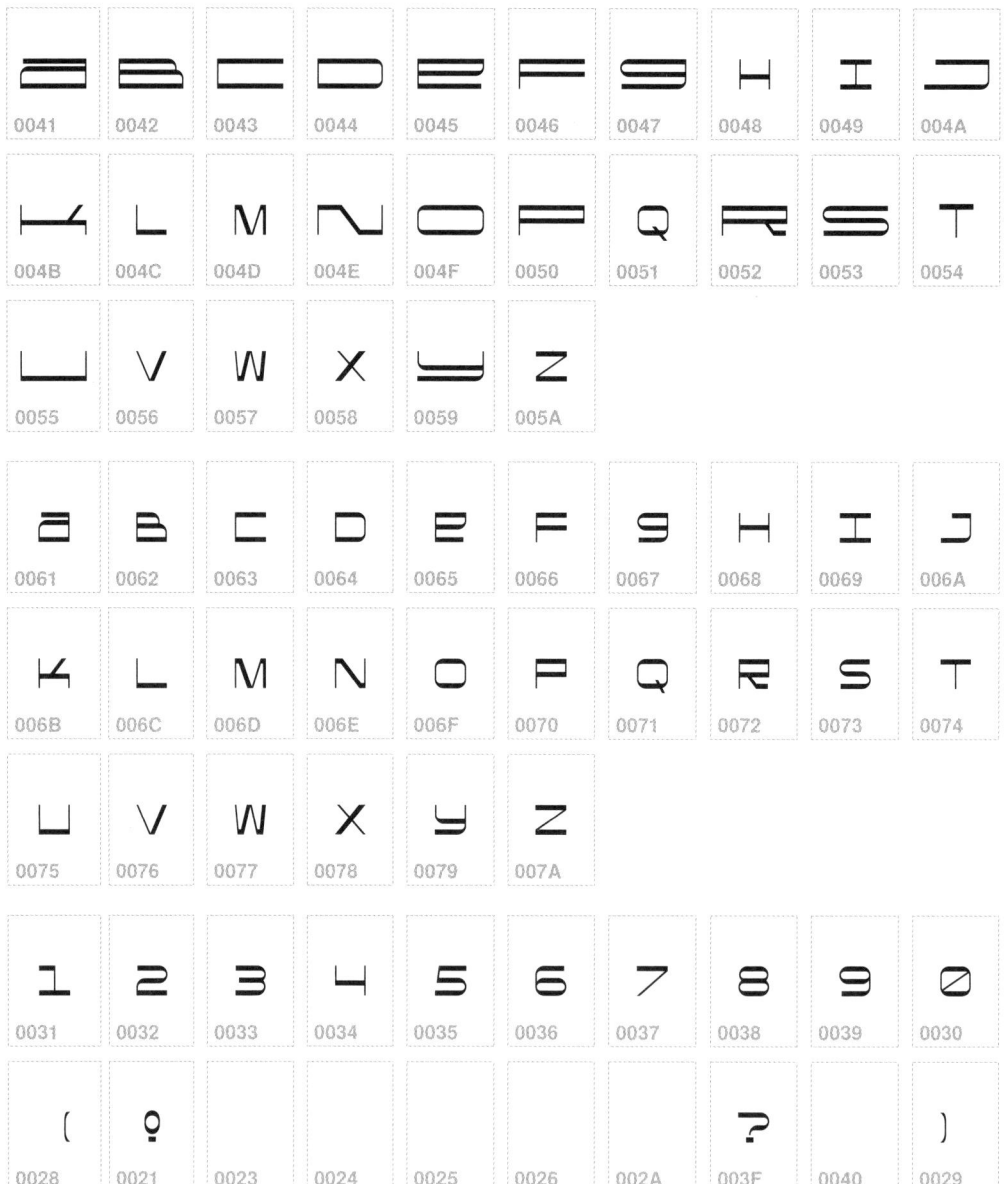

Baptiste
Sophia Brinkgerd

A	B	C	D	E	F	G	H	I	J
0041	0042	0043	0044	0045	0046	0047	0048	0049	004A
K	L	M	N	O	P	Q	R	S	T
004B	004C	004D	004E	004F	0050	0051	0052	0053	0054
U	V	W	X	Y	Z				
0055	0056	0057	0058	0059	005A				
a	b	c	d	e	f	g	h	i	j
0061	0062	0063	0064	0065	0066	0067	0068	0069	006A
k	l	m	n	o	p	q	r	s	t
006B	006C	006D	006E	006F	0070	0071	0072	0073	0074
u	v	w	x	y	z				
0075	0076	0077	0078	0079	007A				
1	2	3	4	5	6	7	8	9	0
0031	0032	0033	0034	0035	0036	0037	0038	0039	0030
(	!	#	§	%	&	*	?	@	)
0028	0021	0023	0024	0025	0026	002A	003F	0040	0029

BedTimes.otf
Gunnar Harrison

A	B	C	D	E	F	G	H	I	J
0041	0042	0043	0044	0045	0046	0047	0048	0049	004A
K	L	M	N	O	P	Q	R	S	T
004B	004C	004D	004E	004F	0050	0051	0052	0053	0054
U	V	W	X	Y	Z				
0055	0056	0057	0058	0059	005A				
a	b	c	d	e	f	g	h	i	j
0061	0062	0063	0064	0065	0066	0067	0068	0069	006A
k	l	m	n	o	p	q	r	s	t
006B	006C	006D	006E	006F	0070	0071	0072	0073	0074
u	v	w	x	y	z				
0075	0076	0077	0078	0079	007A				
1	2	3	4	5	6	7	8	9	0
0031	0032	0033	0034	0035	0036	0037	0038	0039	0030
(	!	#	§	%	&	*	?	@	)
0028	0021	0023	0024	0025	0026	002A	003F	0040	0029

Bigguy
Martin Pyšný

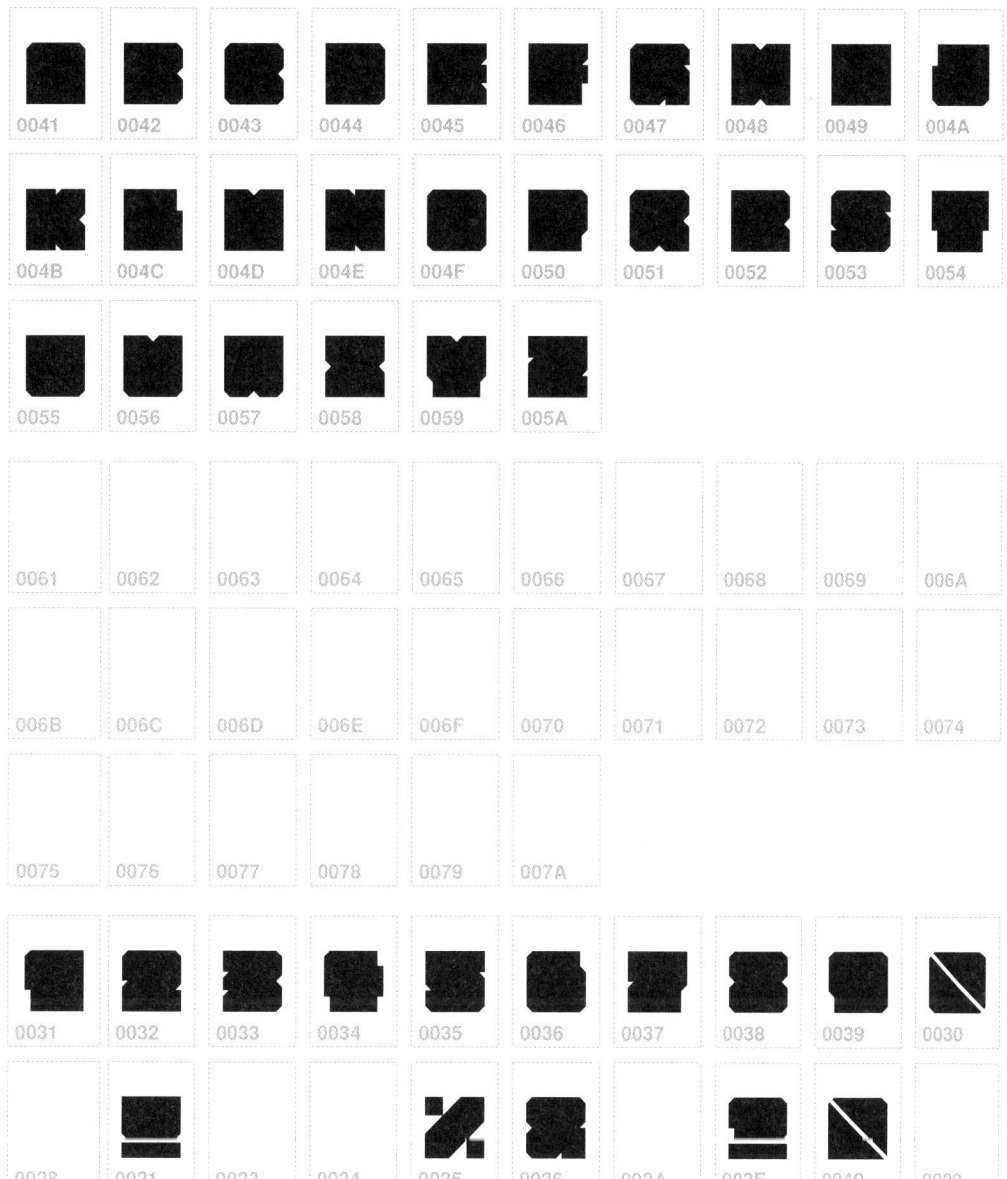

Bonnster
Neville Brody (Brody Associates)

C-Raf
Baptiste Bernazeau

A	B	C	D	E	F	G	H	I	J
0041	0042	0043	0044	0045	0046	0047	0048	0049	004A
K	L	M	N	O	P	Q	R	S	T
004B	004C	004D	004E	004F	0050	0051	0052	0053	0054
U	V	W	X	Y	Z				
0055	0056	0057	0058	0059	005A				
a	b	c	d	e	f	g	h	i	j
0061	0062	0063	0064	0065	0066	0067	0068	0069	006A
k	l	m	n	o	p	q	r	s	t
006B	006C	006D	006E	006F	0070	0071	0072	0073	0074
u	v	w	x	y	z				
0075	0076	0077	0078	0079	007A				
1	2	3	4	5	6	7	8	9	0
0031	0032	0033	0034	0035	0036	0037	0038	0039	0030
(	!				&	*	?		)
0028	0021	0023	0024	0025	0026	002A	003F	0040	0029

Charon
Matthieu Visentin

A	B	C	D	E	F	G	H	I	J
0041	0042	0043	0044	0045	0046	0047	0048	0049	004A
K	L	M	N	O	P	Q	R	S	T
004B	004C	004D	004E	004F	0050	0051	0052	0053	0054
U	V	W	X	Y	Z				
0055	0056	0057	0058	0059	005A				
a	b	c	d	e	f	g	h	i	j
0061	0062	0063	0064	0065	0066	0067	0068	0069	006A
k	l	m	n	o	p	q	r	s	t
006B	006C	006D	006E	006F	0070	0071	0072	0073	0074
u	v	w	x	y	z				
0075	0076	0077	0078	0079	007A				
1	2	3	4	5	6	7	8	9	0
0031	0032	0033	0034	0035	0036	0037	0038	0039	0030
(	!	#	§	%	Я	*	?	@	)
0028	0021	0023	0024	0025	0026	002A	003F	0040	0029

ComicStrip
Paul Bergès

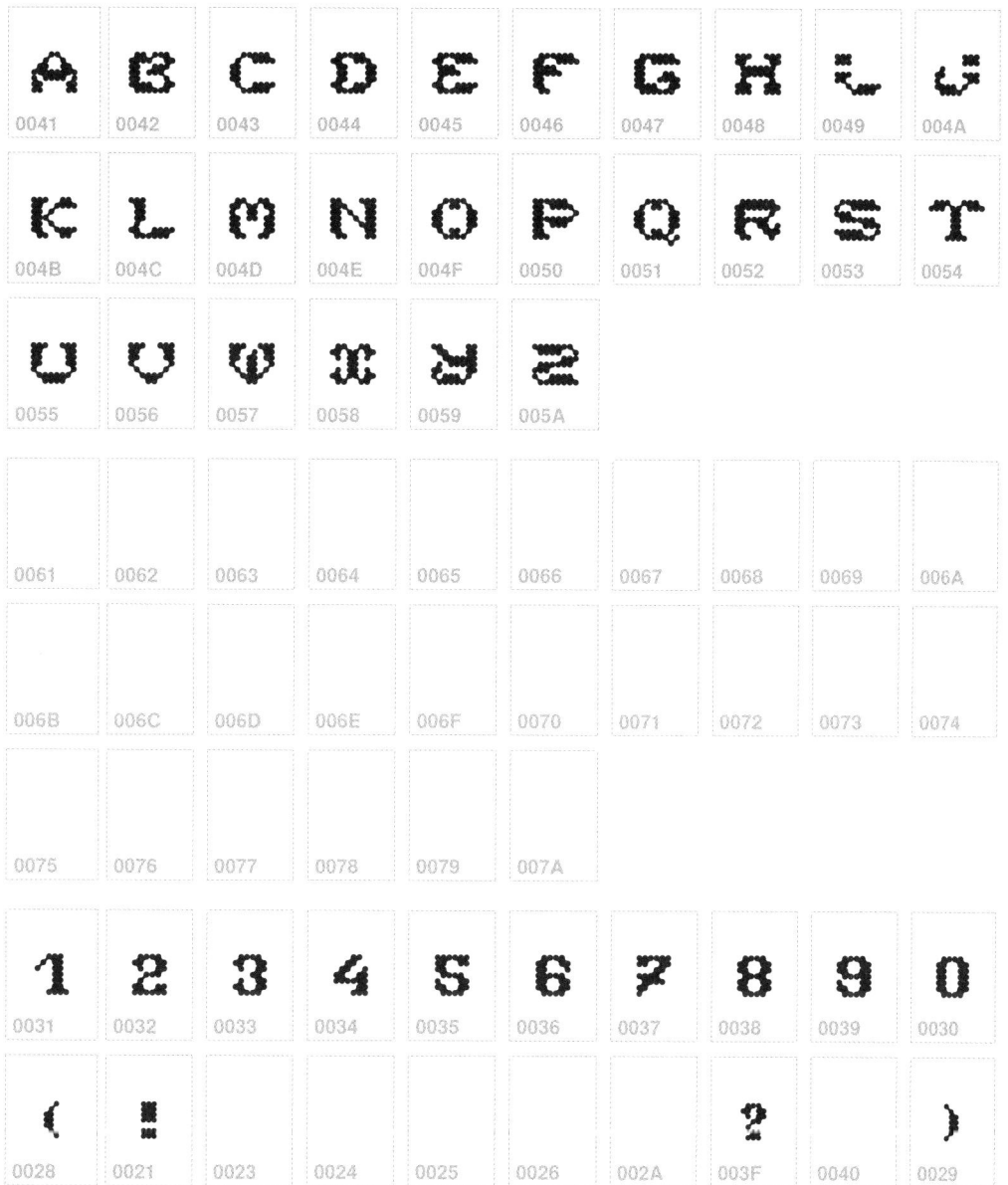

Cosmo
Mingoo Yoon

A	B	C	D	E	F	G	H	I	J
0041	0042	0043	0044	0045	0046	0047	0048	0049	004A
K	L	M	N	O	P	Q	R	S	T
004B	004C	004D	004E	004F	0050	0051	0052	0053	0054
U	V	W	X	Y	Z				
0055	0056	0057	0058	0059	005A				
A	B	C	D	E	F	G	H	I	J
0061	0062	0063	0064	0065	0066	0067	0068	0069	006A
K	L	M	N	O	P	Q	R	S	T
006B	006C	006D	006E	006F	0070	0071	0072	0073	0074
U	V	W	X	Y	Z				
0075	0076	0077	0078	0079	007A				
0031	0032	0033	0034	0035	0036	0037	0038	0039	0030
(	!	#			&	*	?		)
0028	0021	0023	0024	0025	0026	002A	003F	0040	0029

Cryo
Pauline Le Pape

Ⱥ	B	C	D	Ɇ	F	G	H	I	J
0041	0042	0043	0044	0045	0046	0047	0048	0049	004A
K	L	ꟽ	N	O	P	Q	R	S	T
004B	004C	004D	004E	004F	0050	0051	0052	0053	0054
U	V	W	X	Y	Z				
0055	0056	0057	0058	0059	005A				

0061	0062	0063	0064	0065	0066	0067	0068	0069	006A
006B	006C	006D	006E	006F	0070	0071	0072	0073	0074
0075	0076	0077	0078	0079	007A				

1	2	3	4	5	6	7	8	9	0
0031	0032	0033	0034	0035	0036	0037	0038	0039	0030
(	!	#	$	%	&	*	?	@	)
0028	0021	0023	0024	0025	0026	002A	003F	0040	0029

CyberSiberia
Timur Zima

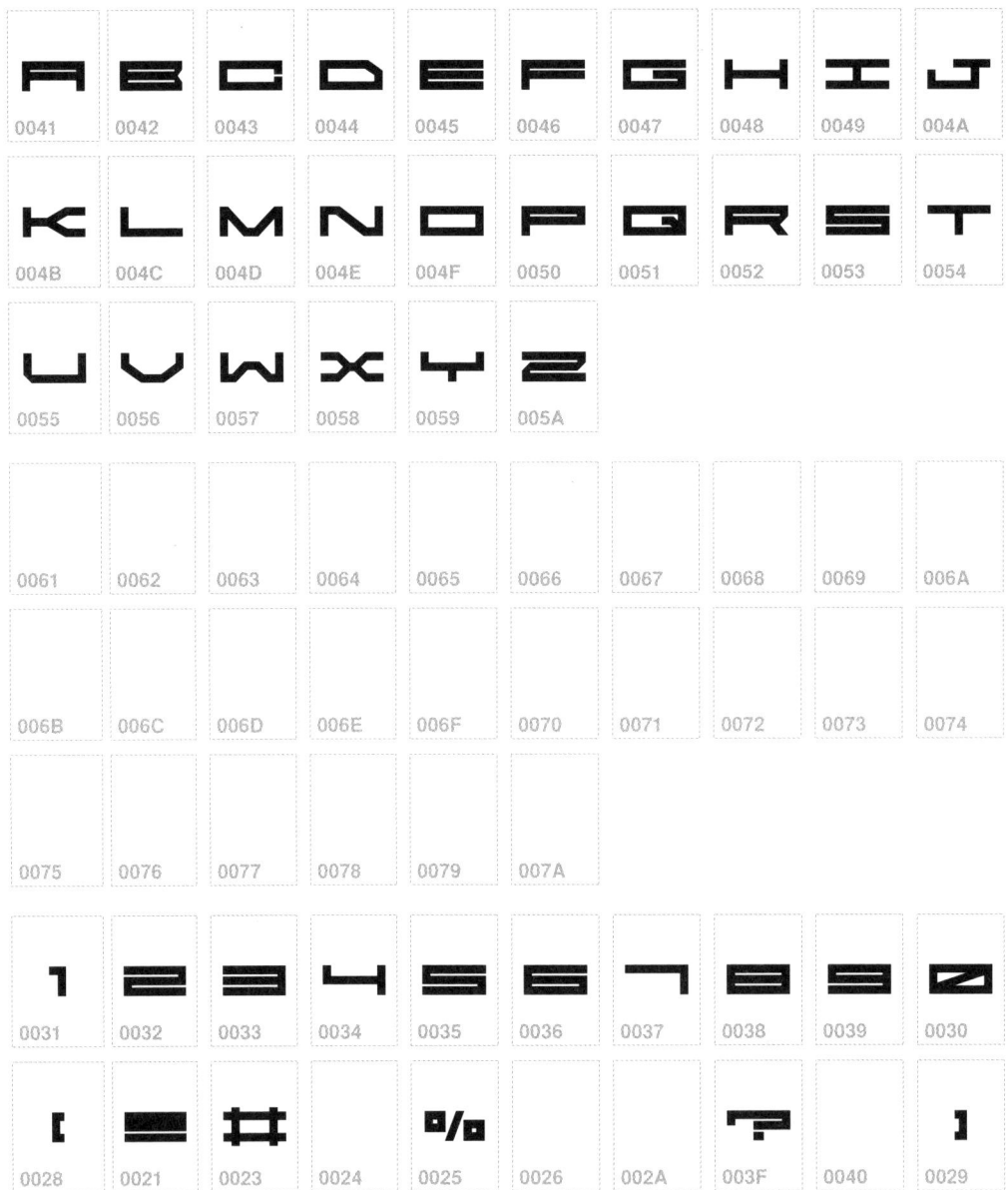

DaVinci
Virgile Flores

A	B	C	D	E	F	G	H	I	J
0041	0042	0043	0044	0045	0046	0047	0048	0049	004A
K	L	M	N	O	P	Q	R	S	T
004B	004C	004D	004E	004F	0050	0051	0052	0053	0054
U	V	W	X	Y	Z				
0055	0056	0057	0058	0059	005A				
a	b	c	d	e	f	g	h	i	j
0061	0062	0063	0064	0065	0066	0067	0068	0069	006A
k	l	m	n	o	p	q	r	s	t
006B	006C	006D	006E	006F	0070	0071	0072	0073	0074
u	v	w	x	y	z				
0075	0076	0077	0078	0079	007A				
1	2	3	4	5	6	7	8	9	0
0031	0032	0033	0034	0035	0036	0037	0038	0039	0030
(	!	#	§	%	&	*	?	@	)
0028	0021	0023	0024	0025	0026	002A	003F	0040	0029

Epingle
Victor Gérard (Various Glyphs)

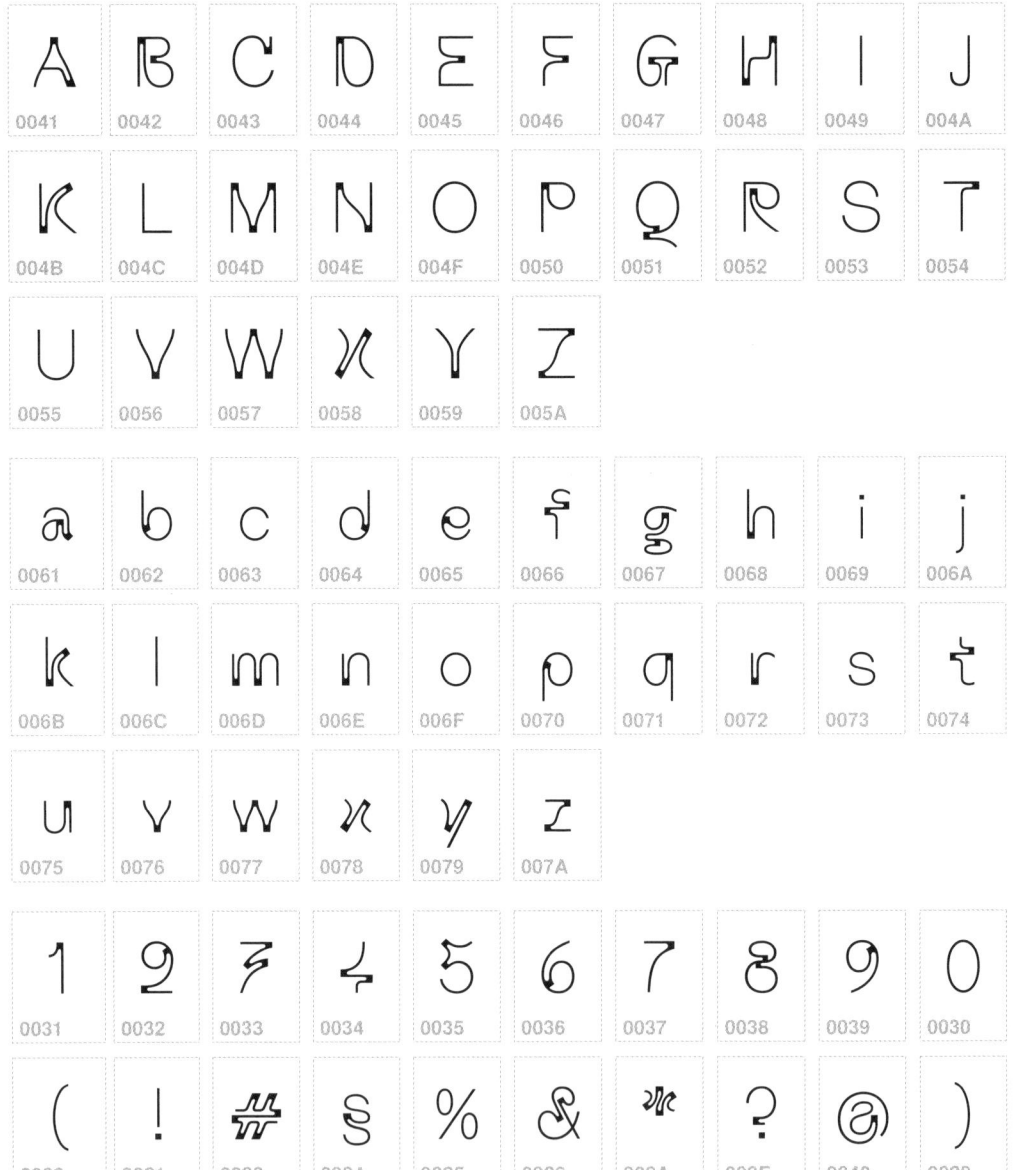

EUPHORIA
Janik Sandbothe

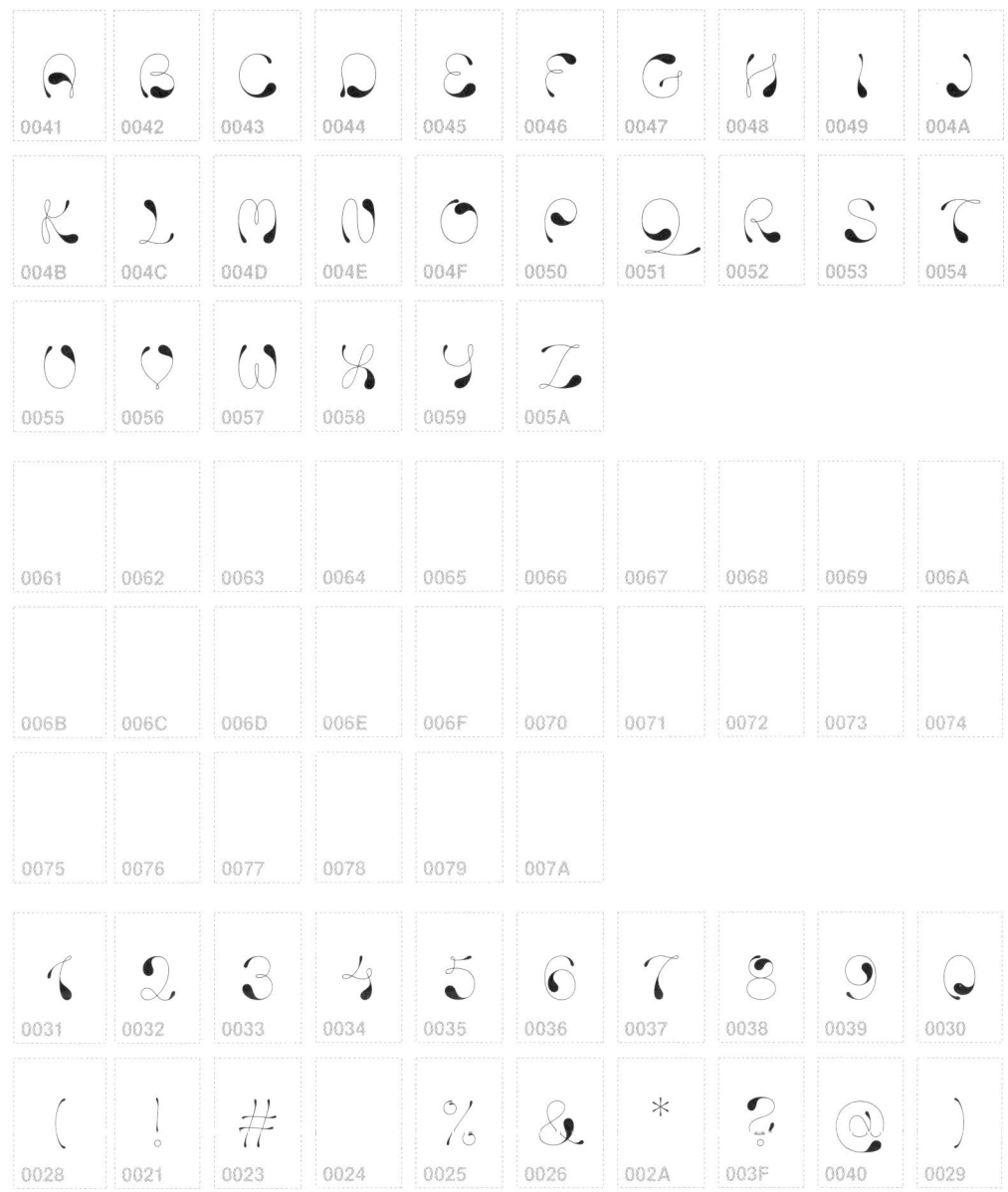

0041	0042	0043	0044	0045	0046	0047	0048	0049	004A
004B	004C	004D	004E	004F	0050	0051	0052	0053	0054
0055	0056	0057	0058	0059	005A				
0061	0062	0063	0064	0065	0066	0067	0068	0069	006A
006B	006C	006D	006E	006F	0070	0071	0072	0073	0074
0075	0076	0077	0078	0079	007A				
0031	0032	0033	0034	0035	0036	0037	0038	0039	0030
0028	0021	0023	0024	0025	0026	002A	003F	0040	0029

Everett
Nolan Paparelli

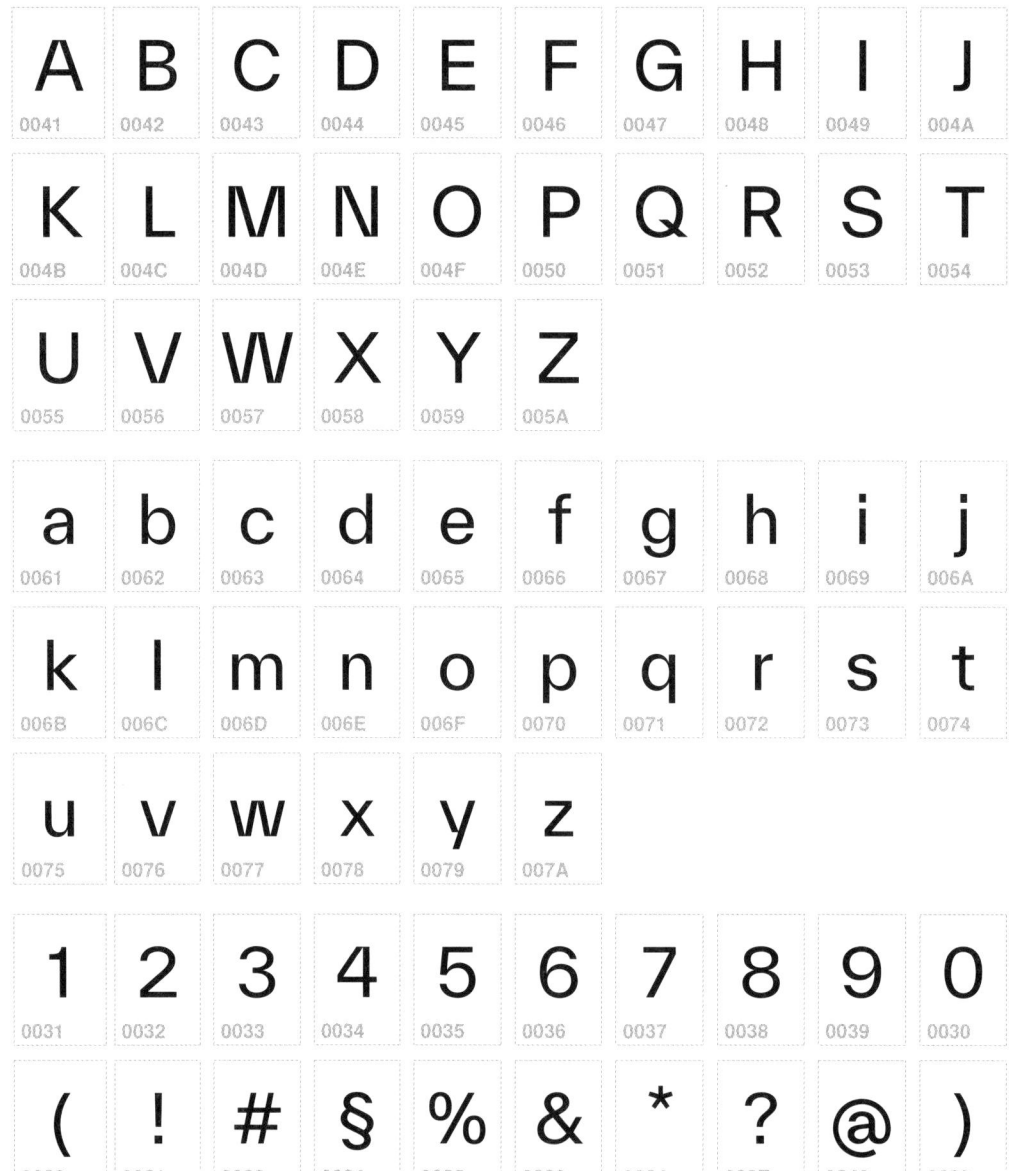

A 0041 B 0042 C 0043 D 0044 E 0045 F 0046 G 0047 H 0048 I 0049 J 004A

K 004B L 004C M 004D N 004E O 004F P 0050 Q 0051 R 0052 S 0053 T 0054

U 0055 V 0056 W 0057 X 0058 Y 0059 Z 005A

a 0061 b 0062 c 0063 d 0064 e 0065 f 0066 g 0067 h 0068 i 0069 j 006A

k 006B l 006C m 006D n 006E o 006F p 0070 q 0071 r 0072 s 0073 t 0074

u 0075 v 0076 w 0077 x 0078 y 0079 z 007A

1 0031 2 0032 3 0033 4 0034 5 0035 6 0036 7 0037 8 0038 9 0039 0 0030

(0028 ! 0021 # 0023 § 0024 % 0025 & 0026 * 002A ? 003F @ 0040) 0029

Eyes
Marie Ducrocq

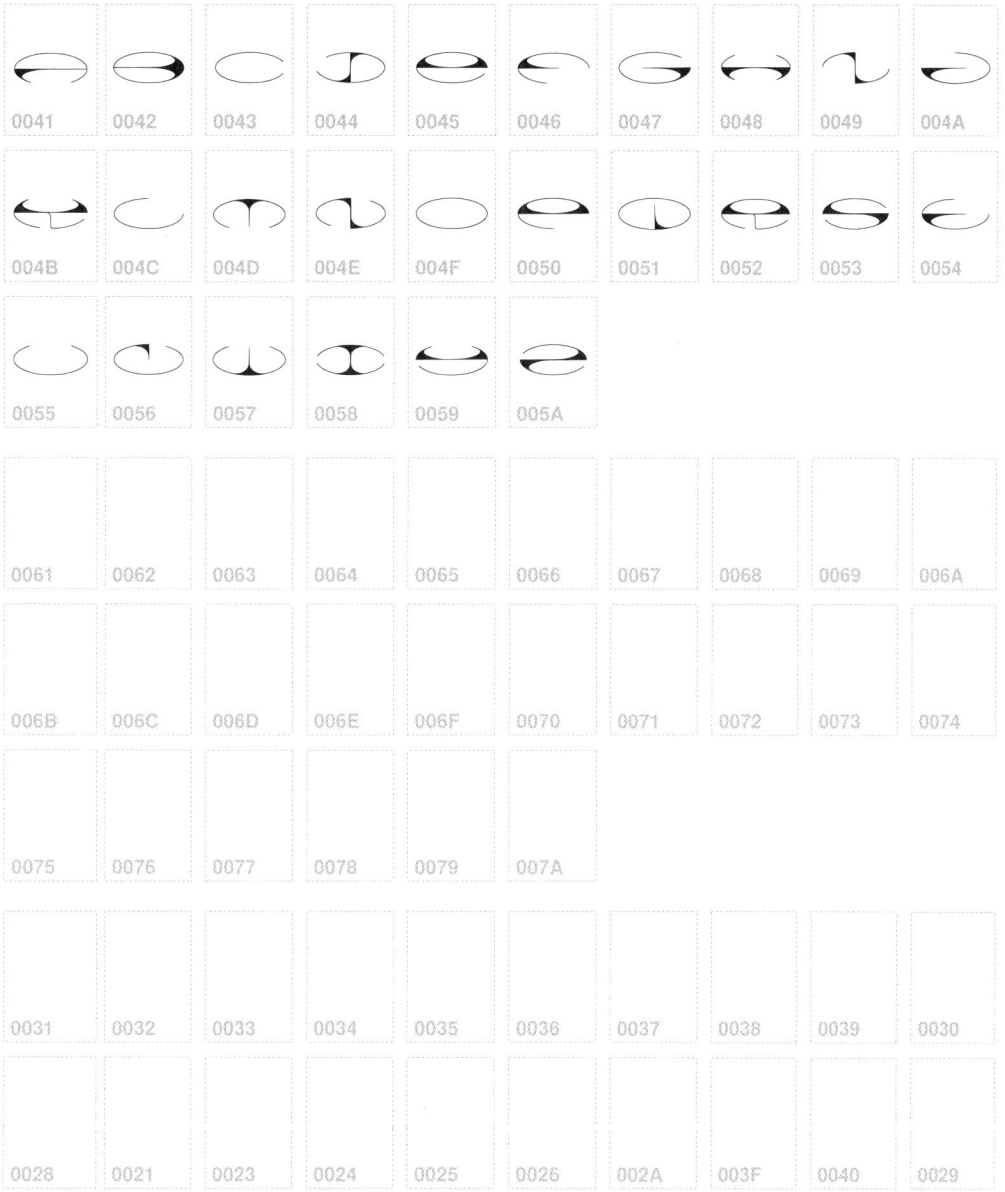

Felsen
Thomas Maier

Gammadion
Laurent Peteuil

0041	0042	0043	0044	0045	0046	0047	0048	0049	004A
004B	004C	004D	004E	004F	0050	0051	0052	0053	0054
0055	0056	0057	0058	0059	005A				
0061	0062	0063	0064	0065	0066	0067	0068	0069	006A
006B	006C	006D	006E	006F	0070	0071	0072	0073	0074
0075	0076	0077	0078	0079	007A				
0031	0032	0033	0034	0035	0036	0037	0038	0039	0030
0028	0021	0023	0024	0025	0026	002A	003F	0040	0029

Gig
Franziska Weitgruber

A	B	C	D	E	F	G	H	I	J
0041	0042	0043	0044	0045	0046	0047	0048	0049	004A
K	L	M	N	O	P	Q	R	S	T
004B	004C	004D	004E	004F	0050	0051	0052	0053	0054
U	V	W	X	Y	Z				
0055	0056	0057	0058	0059	005A				
a	b	c	d	e	f	g	h	i	j
0061	0062	0063	0064	0065	0066	0067	0068	0069	006A
k	l	m	n	o	p	q	r	s	t
006B	006C	006D	006E	006F	0070	0071	0072	0073	0074
u	v	w	x	y	z				
0075	0076	0077	0078	0079	007A				
1	2	3	4	5	6	7	8	9	0
0031	0032	0033	0034	0035	0036	0037	0038	0039	0030
(	!	#	$	%	&	*	?	@	)
0028	0021	0023	0024	0025	0026	002A	003F	0040	0029

Golgotha
Rafael Ribas

A	B	C	D	E	F	G	H	I	J
0041	0042	0043	0044	0045	0046	0047	0048	0049	004A
K	L	M	N	O	P	Q	R	S	T
004B	004C	004D	004E	004F	0050	0051	0052	0053	0054
U	V	W	X	Y	Z				
0055	0056	0057	0058	0059	005A				
a	b	c	d	e	f	g	h	i	j
0061	0062	0063	0064	0065	0066	0067	0068	0069	006A
k	l	m	n	o	p	q	r	s	t
006B	006C	006D	006E	006F	0070	0071	0072	0073	0074
u	v	w	x	y	z				
0075	0076	0077	0078	0079	007A				
1	2	3	4	5	6	7	8	9	0
0031	0032	0033	0034	0035	0036	0037	0038	0039	0030
(	!	#	$	%	&	*	?	@	)
0028	0021	0023	0024	0025	0026	002A	003F	0040	0029

GoilaGoila
Alex Valentina

Gradial
Lena Weber

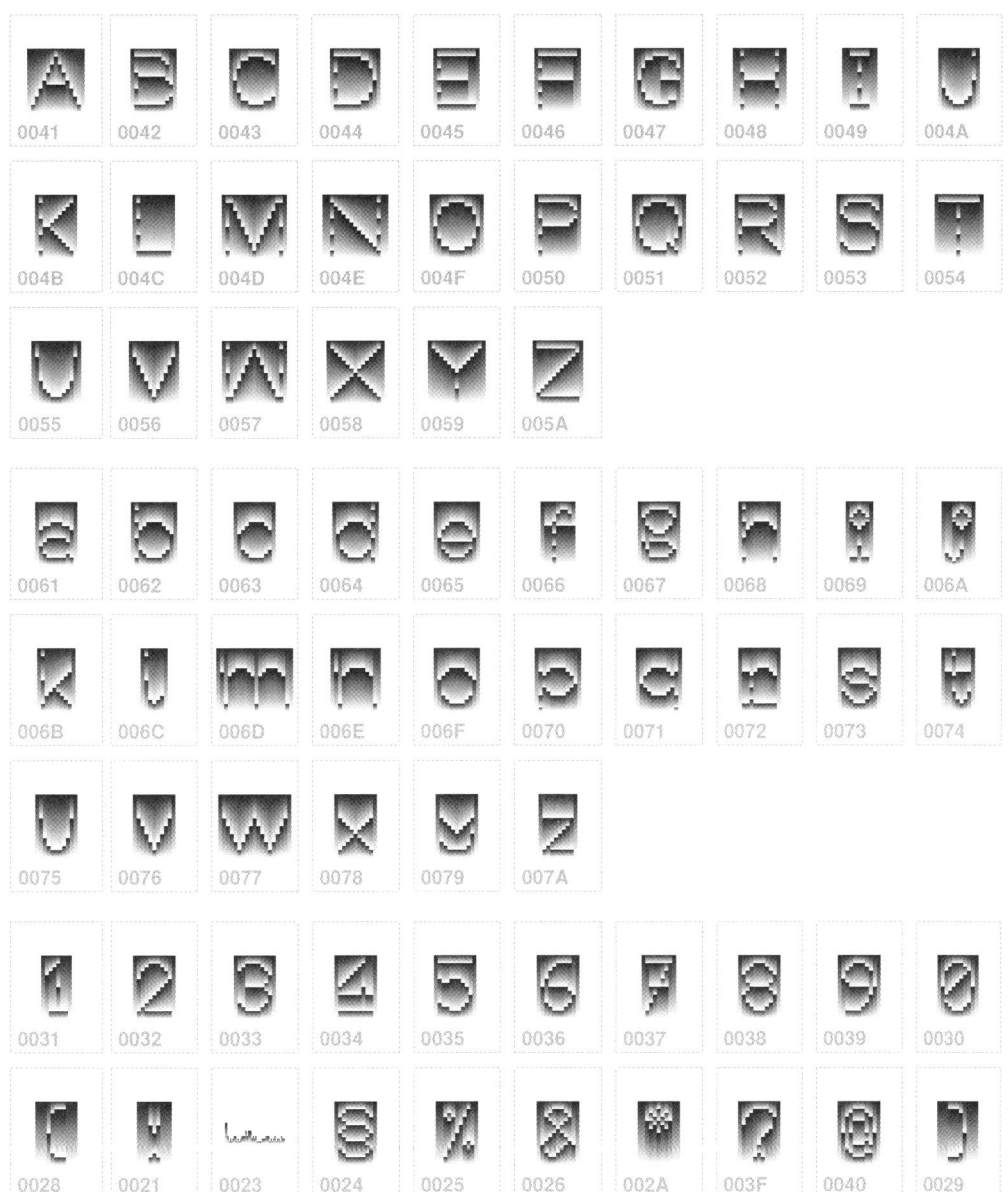

Grand Slang
Nikolas Wrobel

Gray Zone
Youl Joe, Heejae Yang

Gravita
Lena Weber

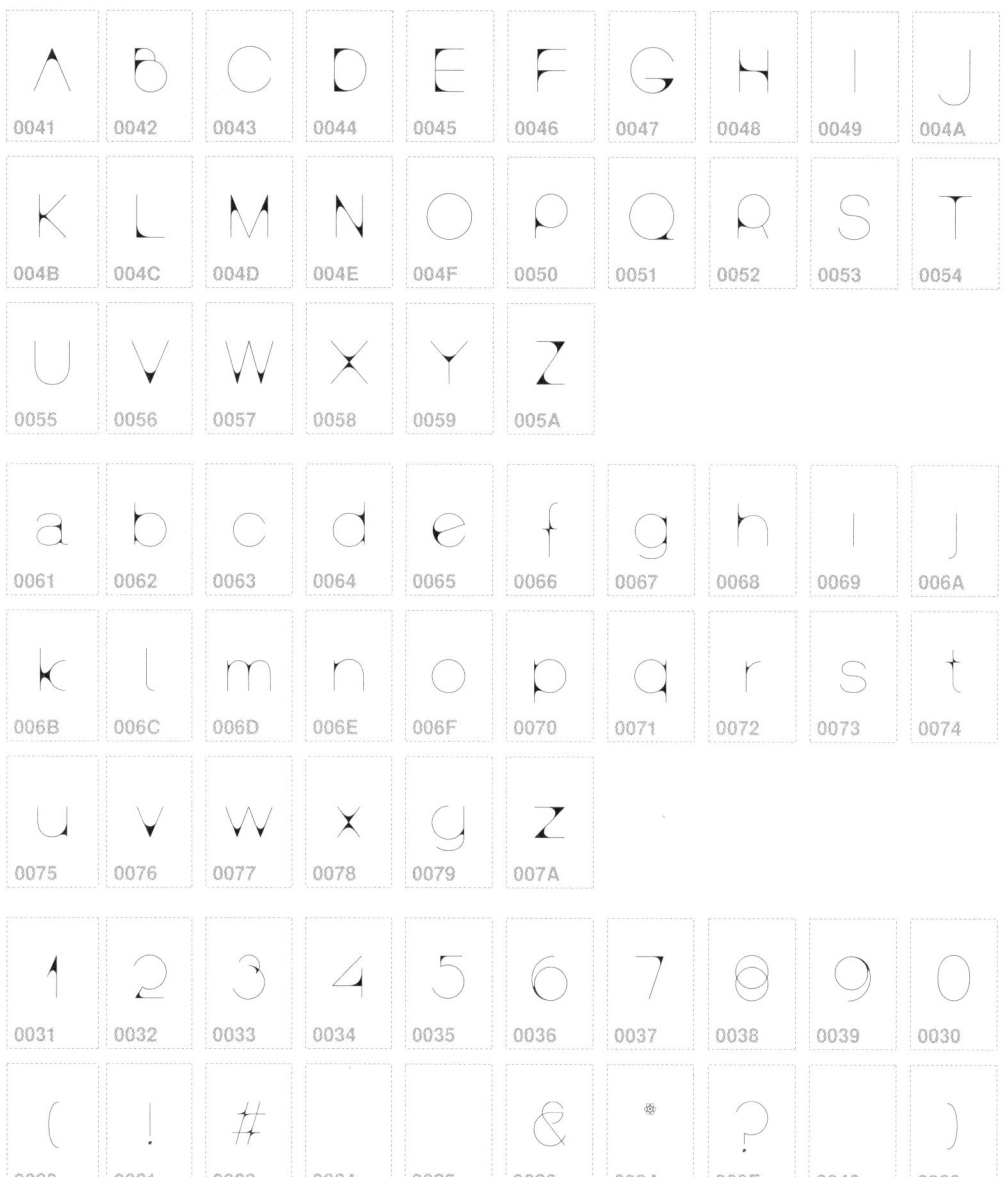

Grotesk Grotesk

Armin Roth, Simon Bork, Lukas Betzler
(studio panorama)

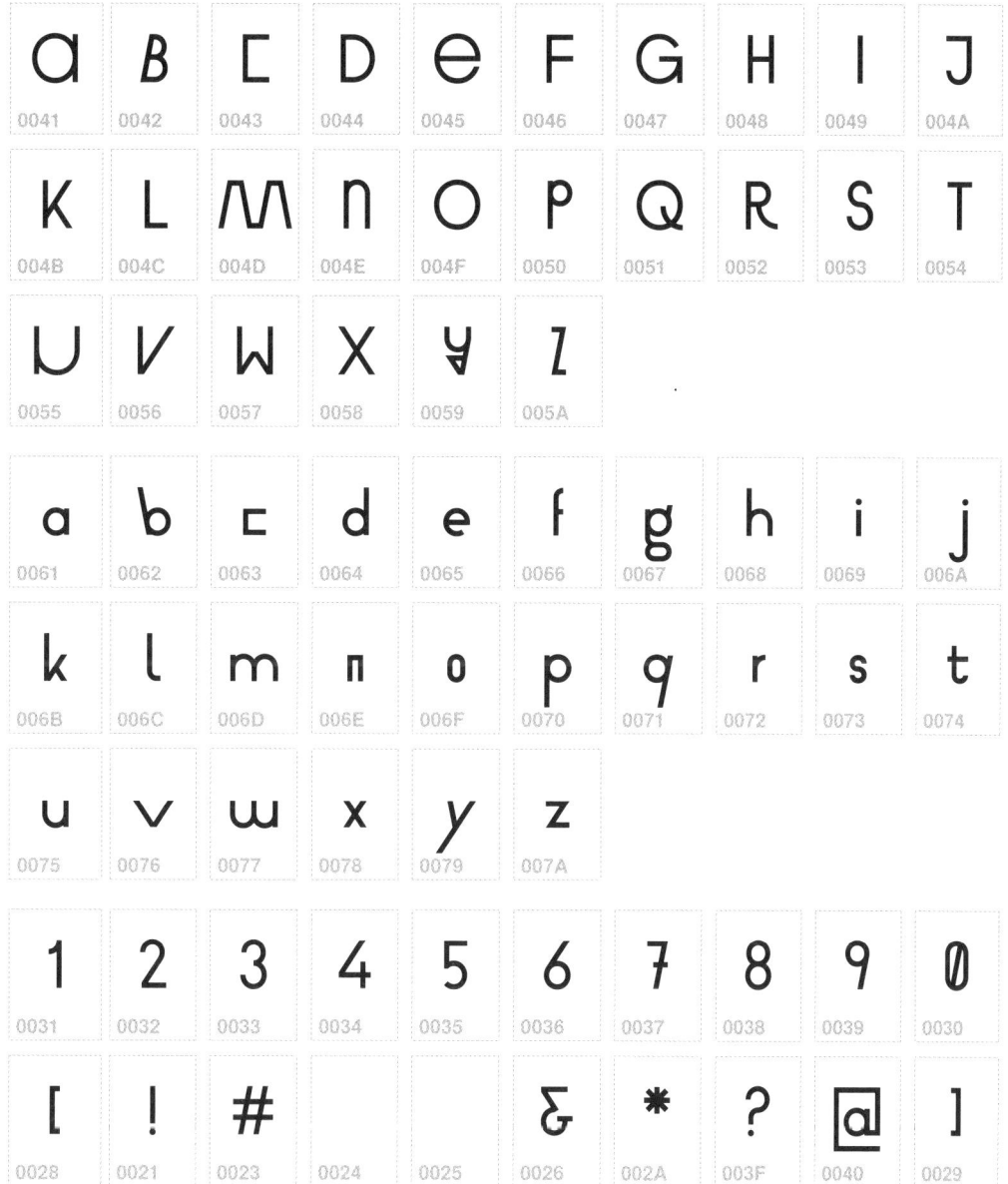

Güggeli
Fabio Biesel

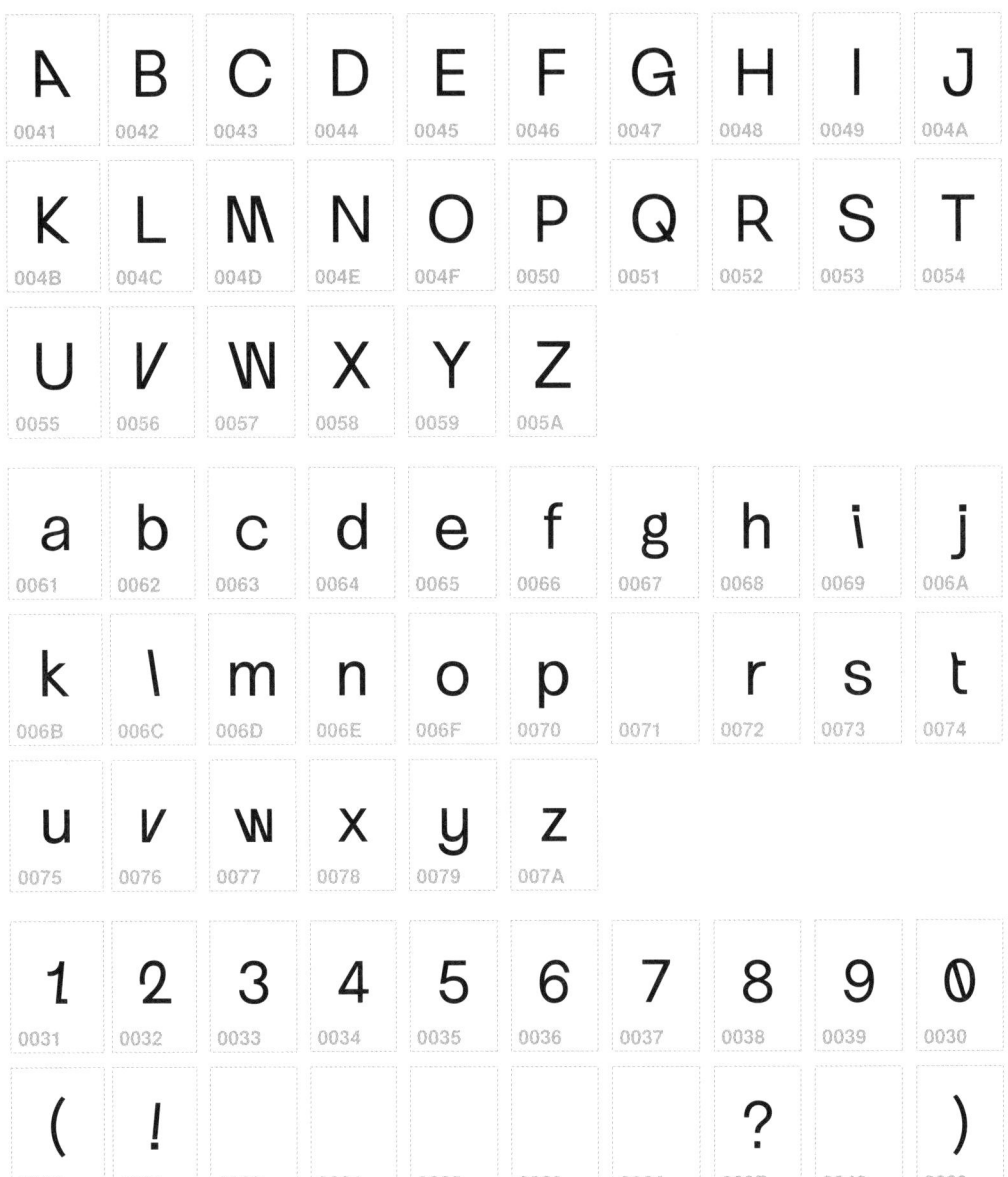

Halunke
Elena Schneider

Heartbeats
Erik Sachse

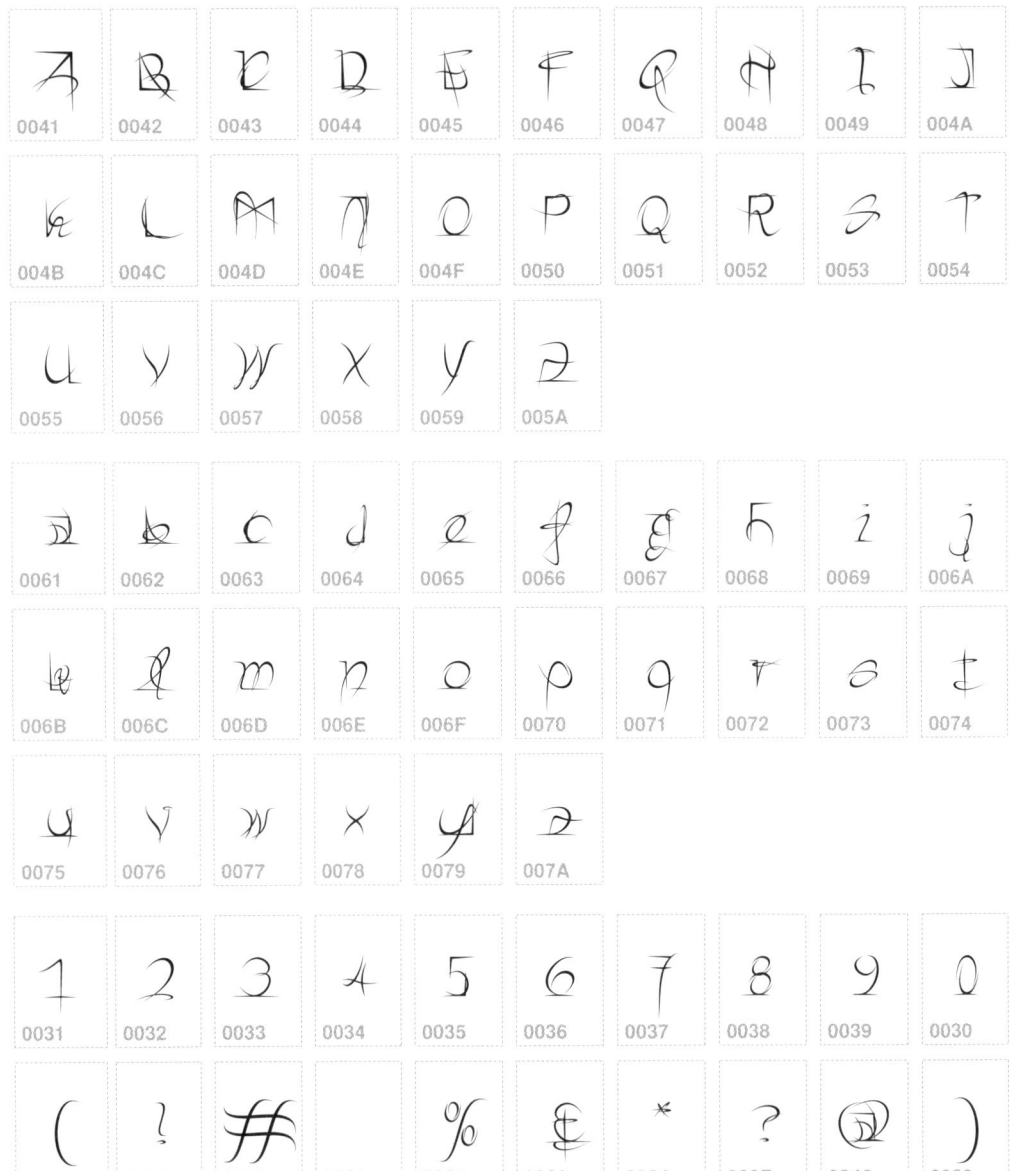

0041	0042	0043	0044	0045	0046	0047	0048	0049	004A
004B	004C	004D	004E	004F	0050	0051	0052	0053	0054
0055	0056	0057	0058	0059	005A				
0061	0062	0063	0064	0065	0066	0067	0068	0069	006A
006B	006C	006D	006E	006F	0070	0071	0072	0073	0074
0075	0076	0077	0078	0079	007A				
0031	0032	0033	0034	0035	0036	0037	0038	0039	0030
0028	0021	0023	0024	0025	0026	002A	003F	0040	0029

Helvetica Blows
Paula Scher, Bruno Bergallo

0041	0042	0043	0044	0045	0046	0047	0048	0049	004A
004B	004C	004D	004E	004F	0050	0051	0052	0053	0054
0055	0056	0057	0058	0059	005A				
0061	0062	0063	0064	0065	0066	0067	0068	0069	006A
006B	006C	006D	006E	006F	0070	0071	0072	0073	0074
0075	0076	0077	0078	0079	007A				
0031	0032	0033	0034	0035	0036	0037	0038	0039	0030
0028	0021	0023	0024	0025	0026	002A	003F	0040	0029

Icarus
Sophia Brinkgerd

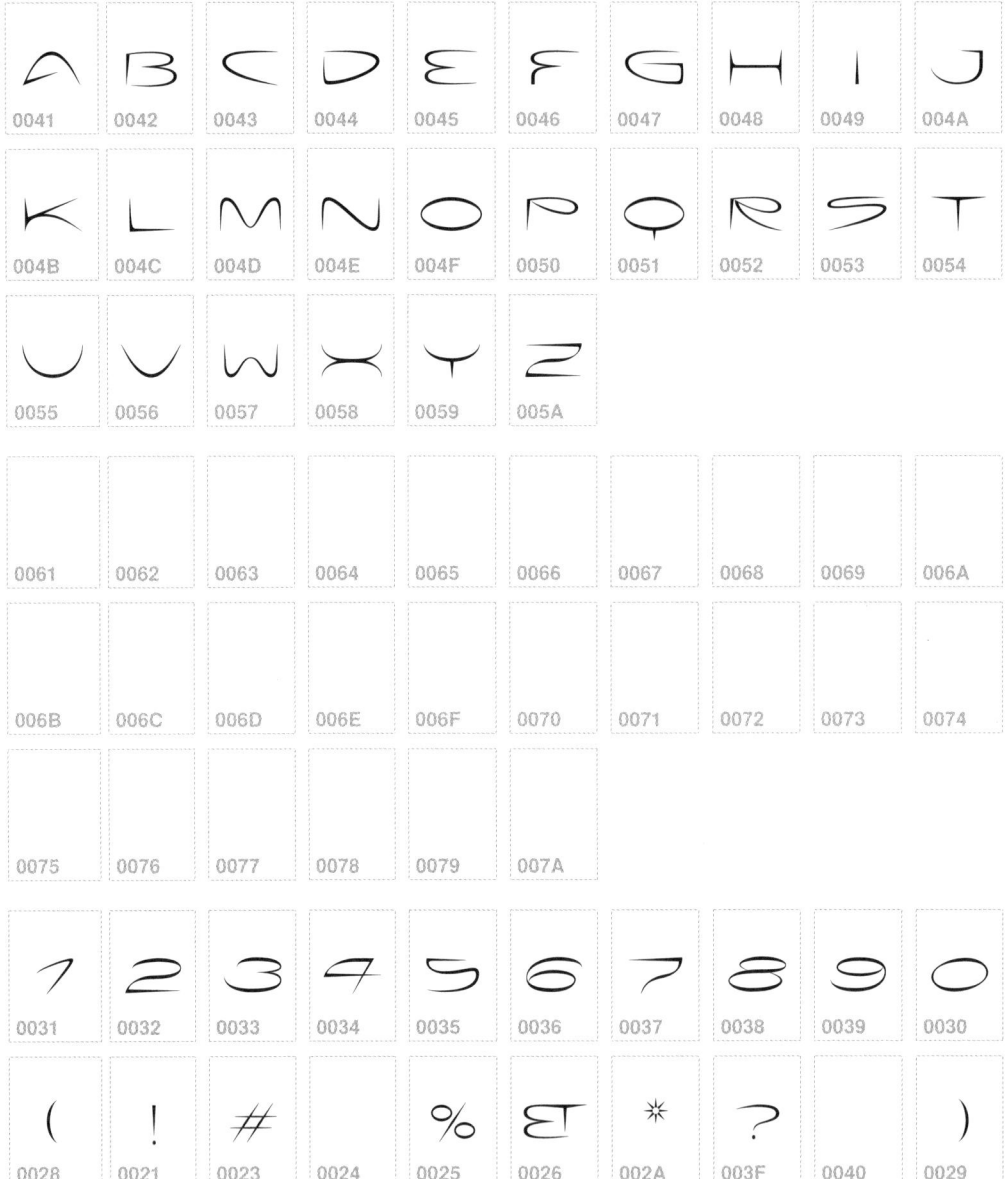

Innschbruck
Daniel Stuhlpfarrer

A	B	C	D	E	F	G	H	I	J
0041	0042	0043	0044	0045	0046	0047	0048	0049	004A
K	L	M	N	O	P	Q	R	S	T
004B	004C	004D	004E	004F	0050	0051	0052	0053	0054
U	V	W	X	Y	Z				
0055	0056	0057	0058	0059	005A				
a	b	c	d	e	f	g	h	i	j
0061	0062	0063	0064	0065	0066	0067	0068	0069	006A
k	l	m	n	o	p	q	r	s	t
006B	006C	006D	006E	006F	0070	0071	0072	0073	0074
u	v	w	x	y	z				
0075	0076	0077	0078	0079	007A				
1	2	3	4	5	6	7	8	9	0
0031	0032	0033	0034	0035	0036	0037	0038	0039	0030
	!						?		
0028	0021	0023	0024	0025	0026	002A	003F	0040	0029

Italica
Sylvain Esposito

A	B	C	D	E	F	G	H	I	J
0041	0042	0043	0044	0045	0046	0047	0048	0049	004A
K	L	M	N	O	P	Q	R	S	T
004B	004C	004D	004E	004F	0050	0051	0052	0053	0054
U	V	W	X	Y	Z				
0055	0056	0057	0058	0059	005A				
a	b	c	d	e	f	g	h	i	j
0061	0062	0063	0064	0065	0066	0067	0068	0069	006A
k	l	m	n	o	p	q	r	s	t
006B	006C	006D	006E	006F	0070	0071	0072	0073	0074
u	v	w	x	y	z				
0075	0076	0077	0078	0079	007A				
0031	0032	0033	0034	0035	0036	0037	0038	0039	0030
	!						?		
0028	0021	0023	0024	0025	0026	002A	003F	0040	0029

Jako
Lisa Petersen

A	B	C	D	E	F	G	H	I	J
0041	0042	0043	0044	0045	0046	0047	0048	0049	004A
K	L	M	N	O	P	Q	R	S	T
004B	004C	004D	004E	004F	0050	0051	0052	0053	0054
U	V	W	X	Y	Z				
0055	0056	0057	0058	0059	005A				
a	b	c	d	e	f	g	h	i	j
0061	0062	0063	0064	0065	0066	0067	0068	0069	006A
k	l	m	n	o	p	q	r	s	t
006B	006C	006D	006E	006F	0070	0071	0072	0073	0074
u	v	w	x	y	z				
0075	0076	0077	0078	0079	007A				
1	2	3	4	5	6	7	8	9	0
0031	0032	0033	0034	0035	0036	0037	0038	0039	0030
(	!						?		)
0028	0021	0023	0024	0025	0026	002A	003F	0040	0029

Jones
Mirko Borsche

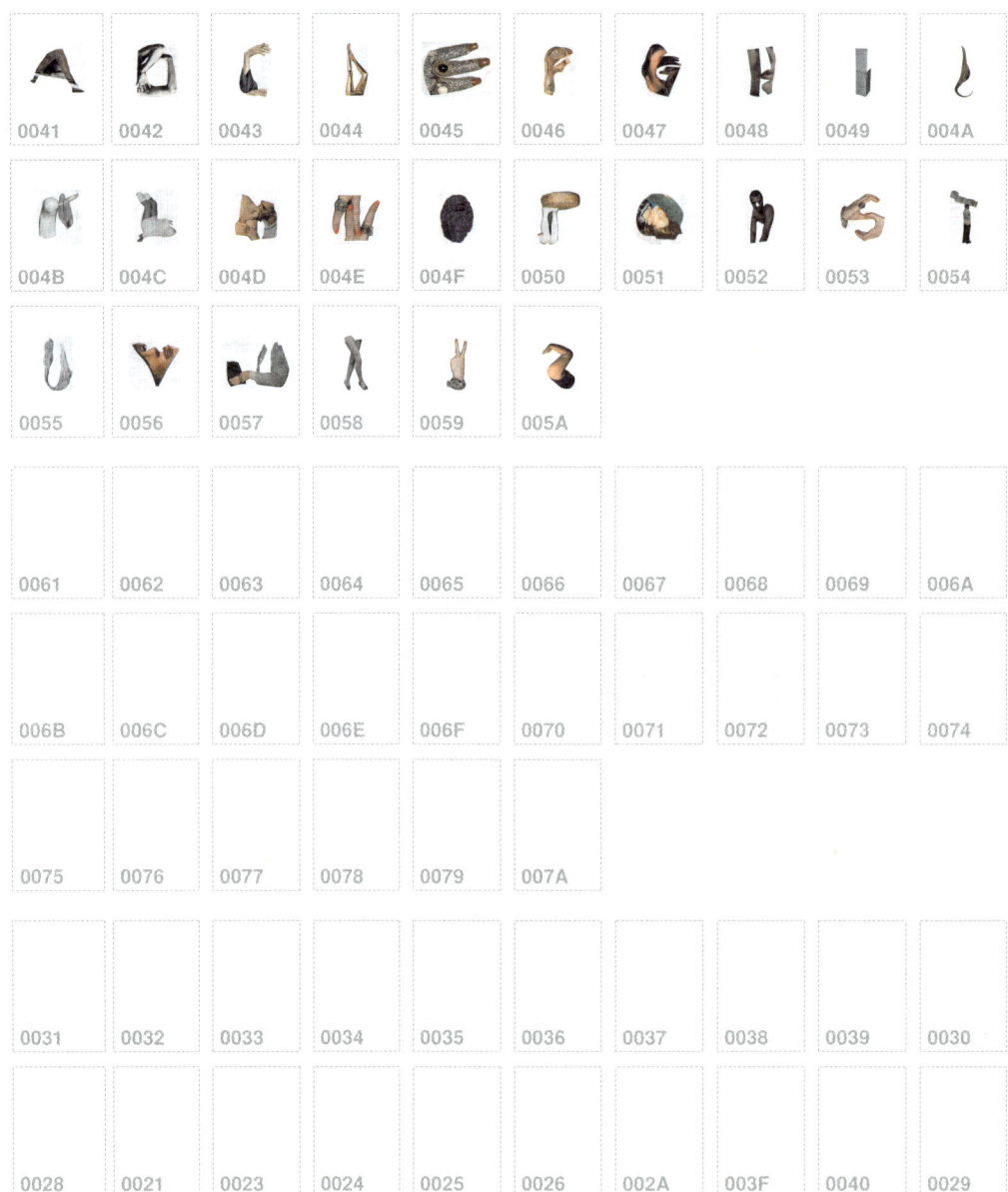

0041	0042	0043	0044	0045	0046	0047	0048	0049	004A
004B	004C	004D	004E	004F	0050	0051	0052	0053	0054
0055	0056	0057	0058	0059	005A				
0061	0062	0063	0064	0065	0066	0067	0068	0069	006A
006B	006C	006D	006E	006F	0070	0071	0072	0073	0074
0075	0076	0077	0078	0079	007A				
0031	0032	0033	0034	0035	0036	0037	0038	0039	0030
0028	0021	0023	0024	0025	0026	002A	003F	0040	0029

Keramika
Mathilde André

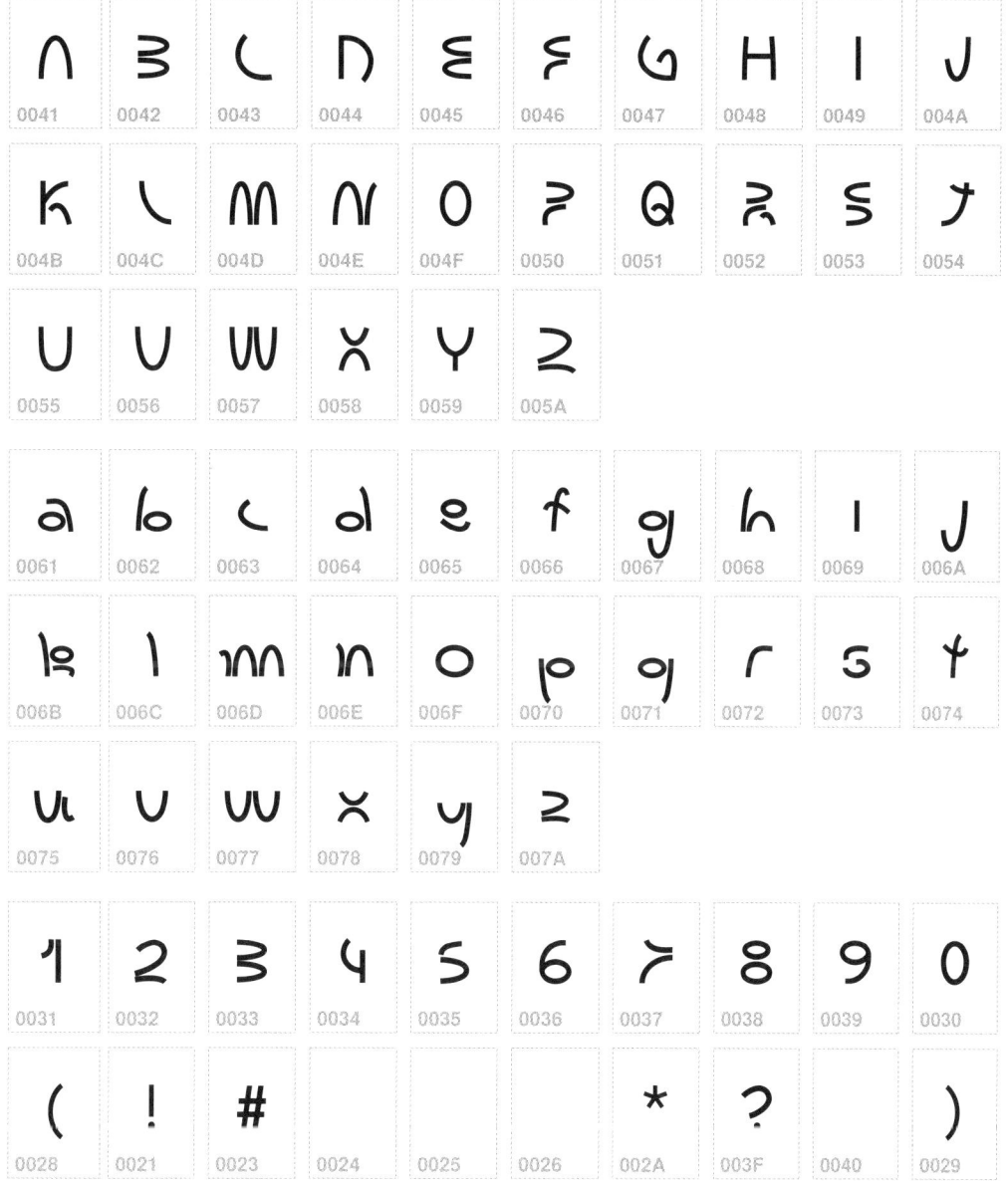

Kevin Fidèle
Isia Yurovsky

A	*B*	*C*	*D*	*E*	*F*	*G*	*H*	*I*	*J*
0041	0042	0043	0044	0045	0046	0047	0048	0049	004A
K	*L*	*M*	*N*	*O*	*P*	*Q*	*R*	*S*	*T*
004B	004C	004D	004E	004F	0050	0051	0052	0053	0054
U	*V*	*W*	*X*	*Y*	*Z*				
0055	0056	0057	0058	0059	005A				
a	*b*	*c*	*d*	*e*	*f*	*g*	*h*	*i*	*j*
0061	0062	0063	0064	0065	0066	0067	0068	0069	006A
k	*l*	*m*	*n*	*o*	*p*	*q*	*r*	*s*	*t*
006B	006C	006D	006E	006F	0070	0071	0072	0073	0074
u	*v*	*w*	*x*	*y*	*z*				
0075	0076	0077	0078	0079	007A				
1	*2*	*3*	*4*	*5*	*6*	*7*	*8*	*9*	*0*
0031	0032	0033	0034	0035	0036	0037	0038	0039	0030
(	*!*	*#*	*§*	*%*	*&*	***	*?*	*@*	*)*
0028	0021	0023	0024	0025	0026	002A	003F	0040	0029

La Nord
Raoul Gottschling

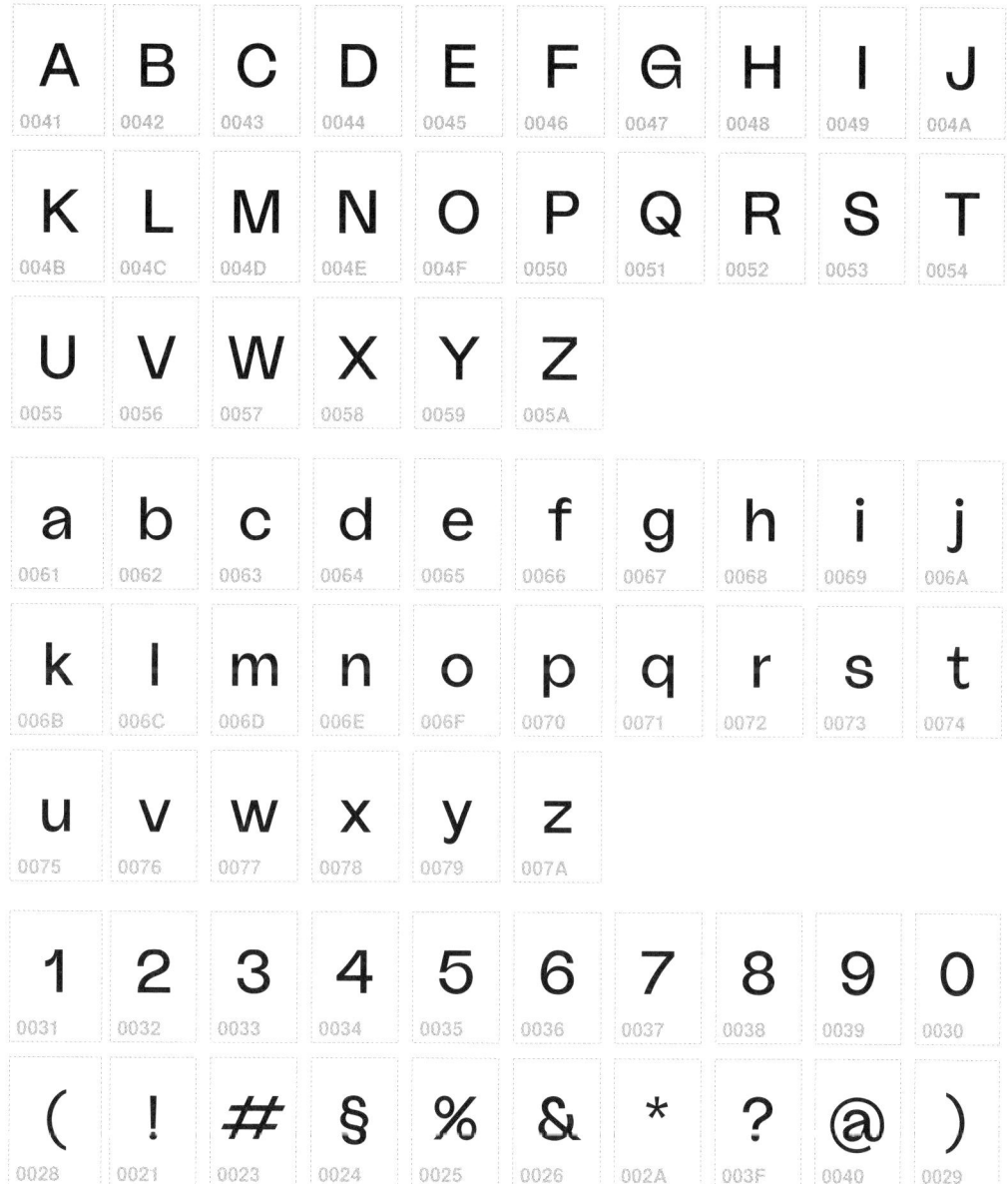

A	B	C	D	E	F	G	H	I	J
0041	0042	0043	0044	0045	0046	0047	0048	0049	004A
K	L	M	N	O	P	Q	R	S	T
004B	004C	004D	004E	004F	0050	0051	0052	0053	0054
U	V	W	X	Y	Z				
0055	0056	0057	0058	0059	005A				
a	b	c	d	e	f	g	h	i	j
0061	0062	0063	0064	0065	0066	0067	0068	0069	006A
k	l	m	n	o	p	q	r	s	t
006B	006C	006D	006E	006F	0070	0071	0072	0073	0074
u	v	w	x	y	z				
0075	0076	0077	0078	0079	007A				
1	2	3	4	5	6	7	8	9	0
0031	0032	0033	0034	0035	0036	0037	0038	0039	0030
(	!	#	§	%	&	*	?	@	)
0028	0021	0023	0024	0025	0026	002A	003F	0040	0029

Langulaire
Loris Pernoux

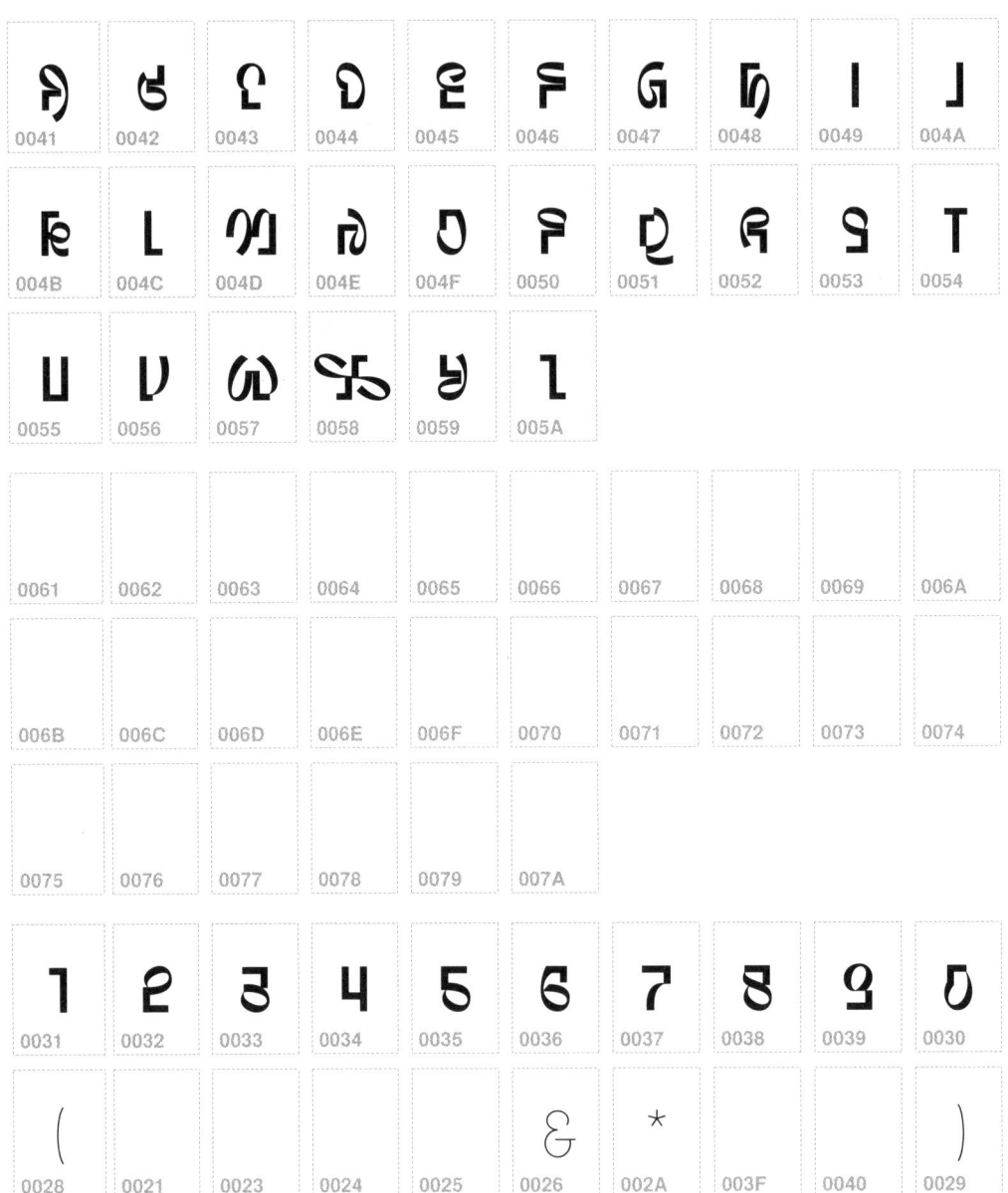

0041	0042	0043	0044	0045	0046	0047	0048	0049	004A
004B	004C	004D	004E	004F	0050	0051	0052	0053	0054
0055	0056	0057	0058	0059	005A				
0061	0062	0063	0064	0065	0066	0067	0068	0069	006A
006B	006C	006D	006E	006F	0070	0071	0072	0073	0074
0075	0076	0077	0078	0079	007A				
0031	0032	0033	0034	0035	0036	0037	0038	0039	0030
0028	0021	0023	0024	0025	0026	002A	003F	0040	0029

Lapicide
Emilie Vizcano

A	B	C	D	E	F	G	H	I	J
0041	0042	0043	0044	0045	0046	0047	0048	0049	004A
K	L	M	N	O	P	Q	R	S	T
004B	004C	004D	004E	004F	0050	0051	0052	0053	0054
U	V	W	X	Y	Z				
0055	0056	0057	0058	0059	005A				
a	b	c	d	e	f	g	h	i	j
0061	0062	0063	0064	0065	0066	0067	0068	0069	006A
k	l	m	n	o	p	q	r	s	t
006B	006C	006D	006E	006F	0070	0071	0072	0073	0074
u	v	w	x	y	z				
0075	0076	0077	0078	0079	007A				
1	2	3	4	5	6	7	8	9	0
0031	0032	0033	0034	0035	0036	0037	0038	0039	0030
(	!	#	§	%	&	*	?	@	)
0028	0021	0023	0024	0025	0026	002A	003F	0040	0029

Lausanne
Nizar Kazan

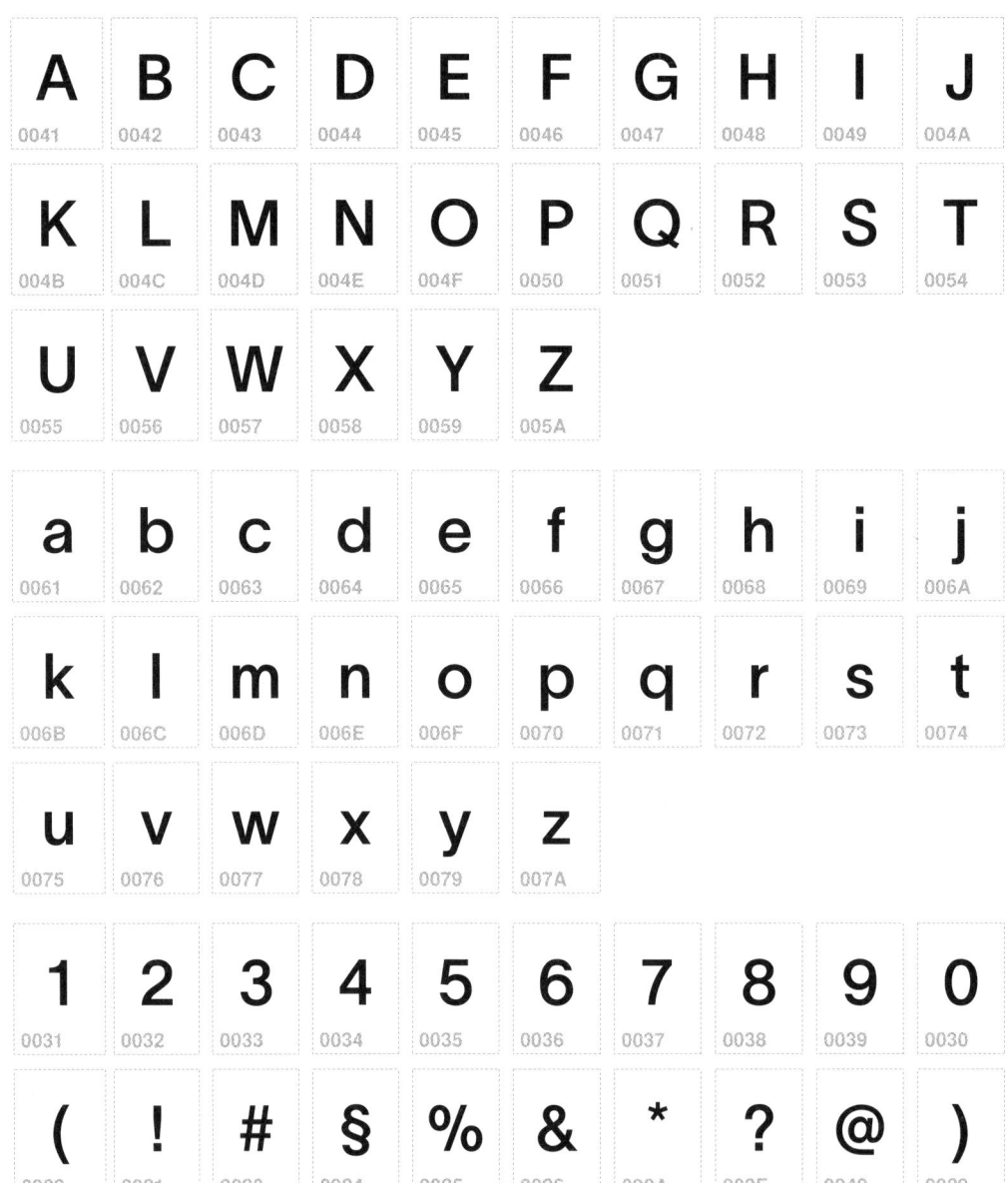

A	B	C	D	E	F	G	H	I	J
0041	0042	0043	0044	0045	0046	0047	0048	0049	004A
K	L	M	N	O	P	Q	R	S	T
004B	004C	004D	004E	004F	0050	0051	0052	0053	0054
U	V	W	X	Y	Z				
0055	0056	0057	0058	0059	005A				
a	b	c	d	e	f	g	h	i	j
0061	0062	0063	0064	0065	0066	0067	0068	0069	006A
k	l	m	n	o	p	q	r	s	t
006B	006C	006D	006E	006F	0070	0071	0072	0073	0074
u	v	w	x	y	z				
0075	0076	0077	0078	0079	007A				
1	2	3	4	5	6	7	8	9	0
0031	0032	0033	0034	0035	0036	0037	0038	0039	0030
(	!	#	§	%	&	*	?	@	)
0028	0021	0023	0024	0025	0026	002A	003F	0040	0029

Lil Thug
Brando Corradini

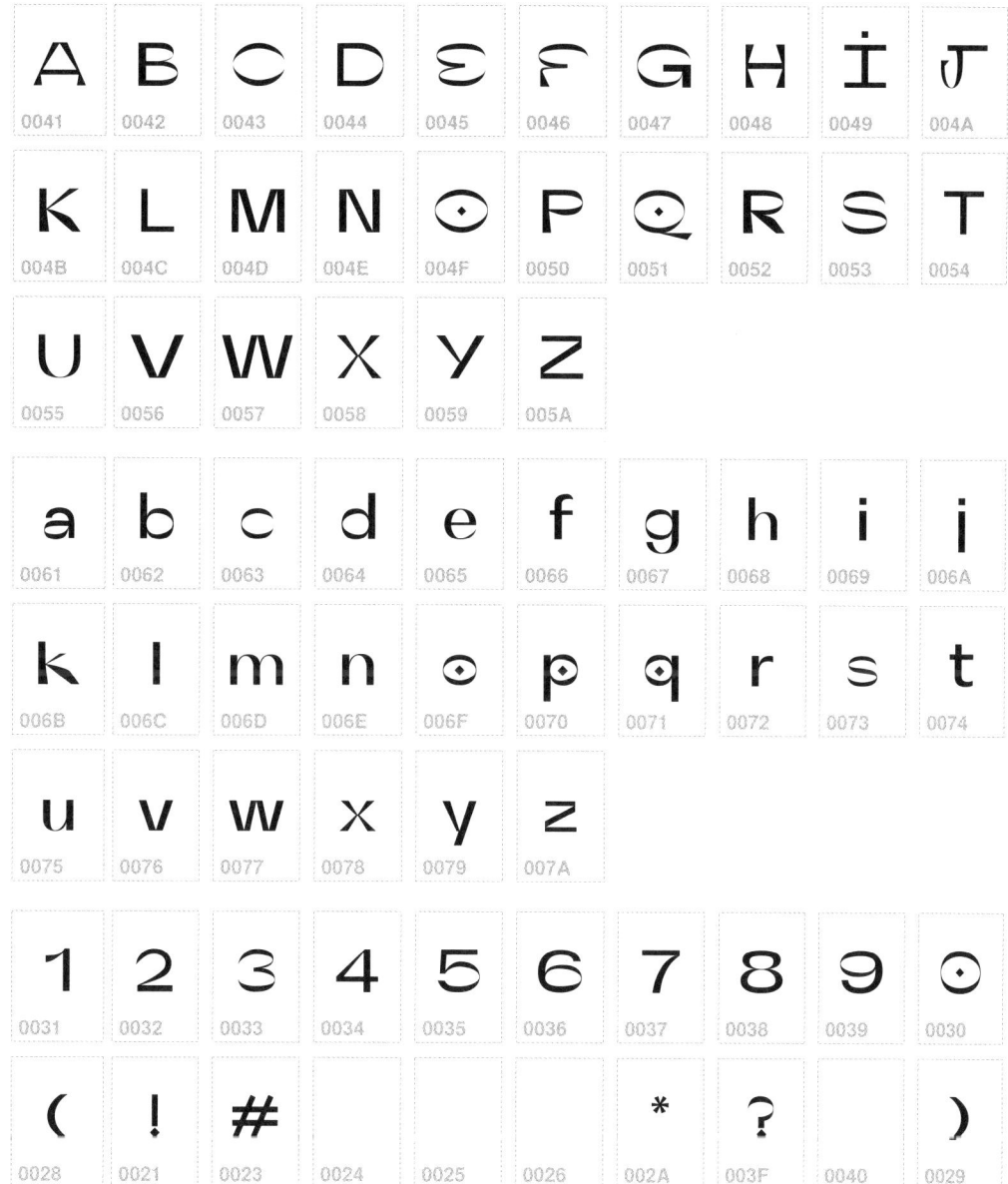

Line
Sepus Noordmans (Parabol Studio)

LLUNA

Sara Bastai

0041	0042	0043	0044	0045	0046	0047	0048	0049	004A
004B	004C	004D	004E	004F	0050	0051	0052	0053	0054
0055	0056	0057	0058	0059	005A				

a	b	c	d	e	f	g	h	i	j
0061	0062	0063	0064	0065	0066	0067	0068	0069	006A
k	l	m	n	o	p	q	r	s	t
006B	006C	006D	006E	006F	0070	0071	0072	0073	0074
u	v	w	z	y	s				
0075	0076	0077	0078	0079	007A				

0031	0032	0033	0034	0035	0036	0037	0038	0039	0030
0028	0021	0023	0024	0025	0026	002A	003F	0040	0029

MD Maya
Moby Digg

0041	0042	0043	0044	0045	0046	0047	0048	0049	004A
004B	004C	004D	004E	004F	0050	0051	0052	0053	0054
0055	0056	0057	0058	0059	005A				
0061	0062	0063	0064	0065	0066	0067	0068	0069	006A
006B	006C	006D	006E	006F	0070	0071	0072	0073	0074
0075	0076	0077	0078	0079	007A				
0031	0032	0033	0034	0035	0036	0037	0038	0039	0030
0028	0021	0023	0024	0025	0026	002A	003F	0040	0029

Mercial
Luca Pellegrini

A	B	C	D	E	F	G	H	I	J
0041	0042	0043	0044	0045	0046	0047	0048	0049	004A
K	L	M	N	O	P	Q	R	S	T
004B	004C	004D	004E	004F	0050	0051	0052	0053	0054
U	V	W	X	Y	Z				
0055	0056	0057	0058	0059	005A				
a	b	c	d	e	f	g	h	i	j
0061	0062	0063	0064	0065	0066	0067	0068	0069	006A
k	l	m	n	o	p	q	r	s	t
006B	006C	006D	006E	006F	0070	0071	0072	0073	0074
u	v	w	x	y	z				
0075	0076	0077	0078	0079	007A				
1	2	3	4	5	6	7	8	9	0
0031	0032	0033	0034	0035	0036	0037	0038	0039	0030
(	!	#	§	%	&	*	?	@	)
0028	0021	0023	0024	0025	0026	002A	003F	0040	0029

Messapia
Luca Marsano (Collletttivo)

A	B	C	D	E	F	G	H	I	J
0041	0042	0043	0044	0045	0046	0047	0048	0049	004A
K	L	M	N	O	P	Q	R	S	T
004B	004C	004D	004E	004F	0050	0051	0052	0053	0054
U	V	W	X	Y	Z				
0055	0056	0057	0058	0059	005A				
a	b	c	d	e	f	g	h	i	j
0061	0062	0063	0064	0065	0066	0067	0068	0069	006A
k	l	m	n	o	p	q	r	s	t
006B	006C	006D	006E	006F	0070	0071	0072	0073	0074
u	v	w	x	y	z				
0075	0076	0077	0078	0079	007A				
1	2	3	4	5	6	7	8	9	0
0031	0032	0033	0034	0035	0036	0037	0038	0039	0030
(	!	#	§	%	&	*	?	@	)
0028	0021	0023	0024	0025	0026	002A	003F	0040	0029

Mihara
Kia Tasbihgou

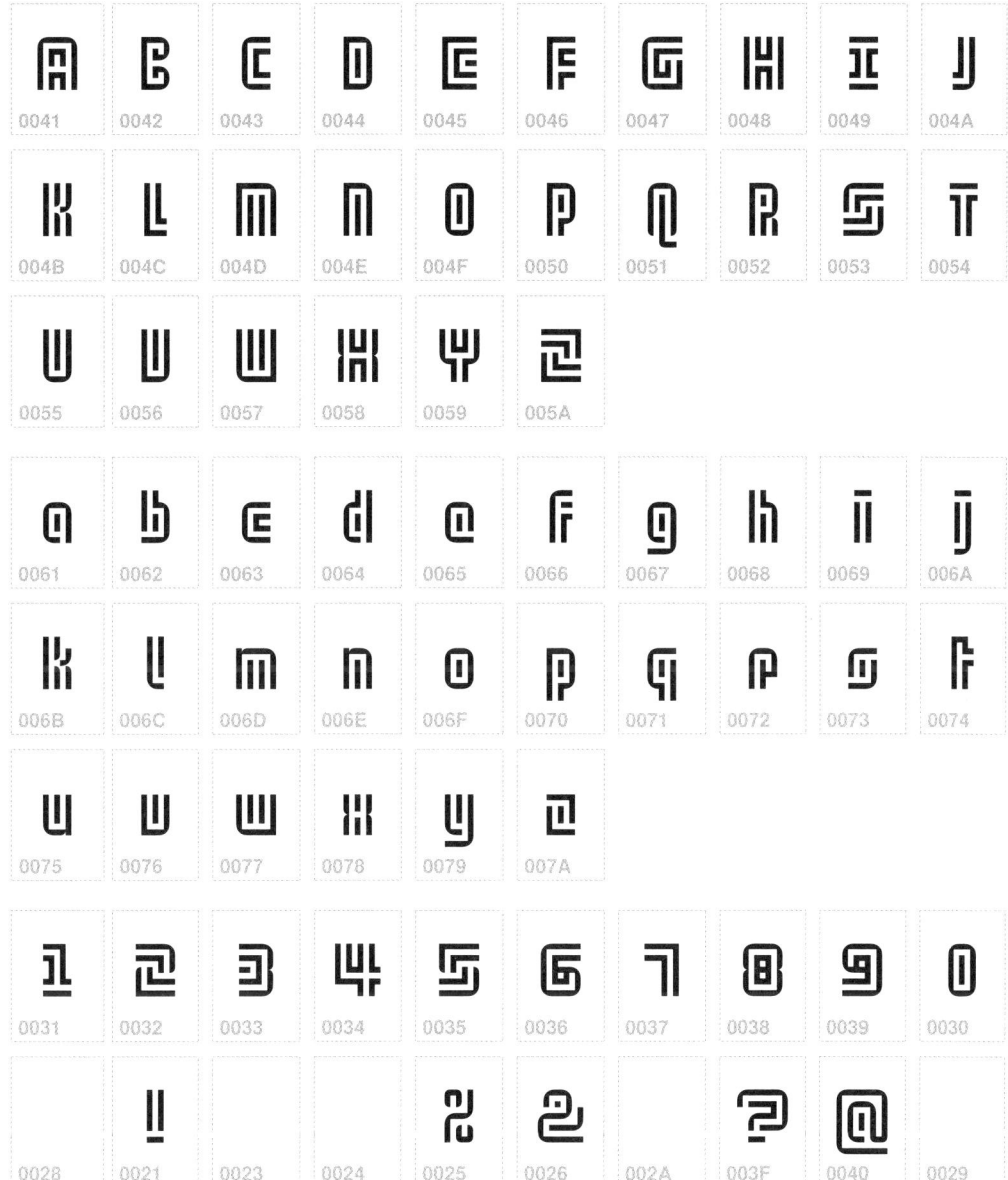

Modal
Stefanie Vogl

Molody
Tatjana Pöschke

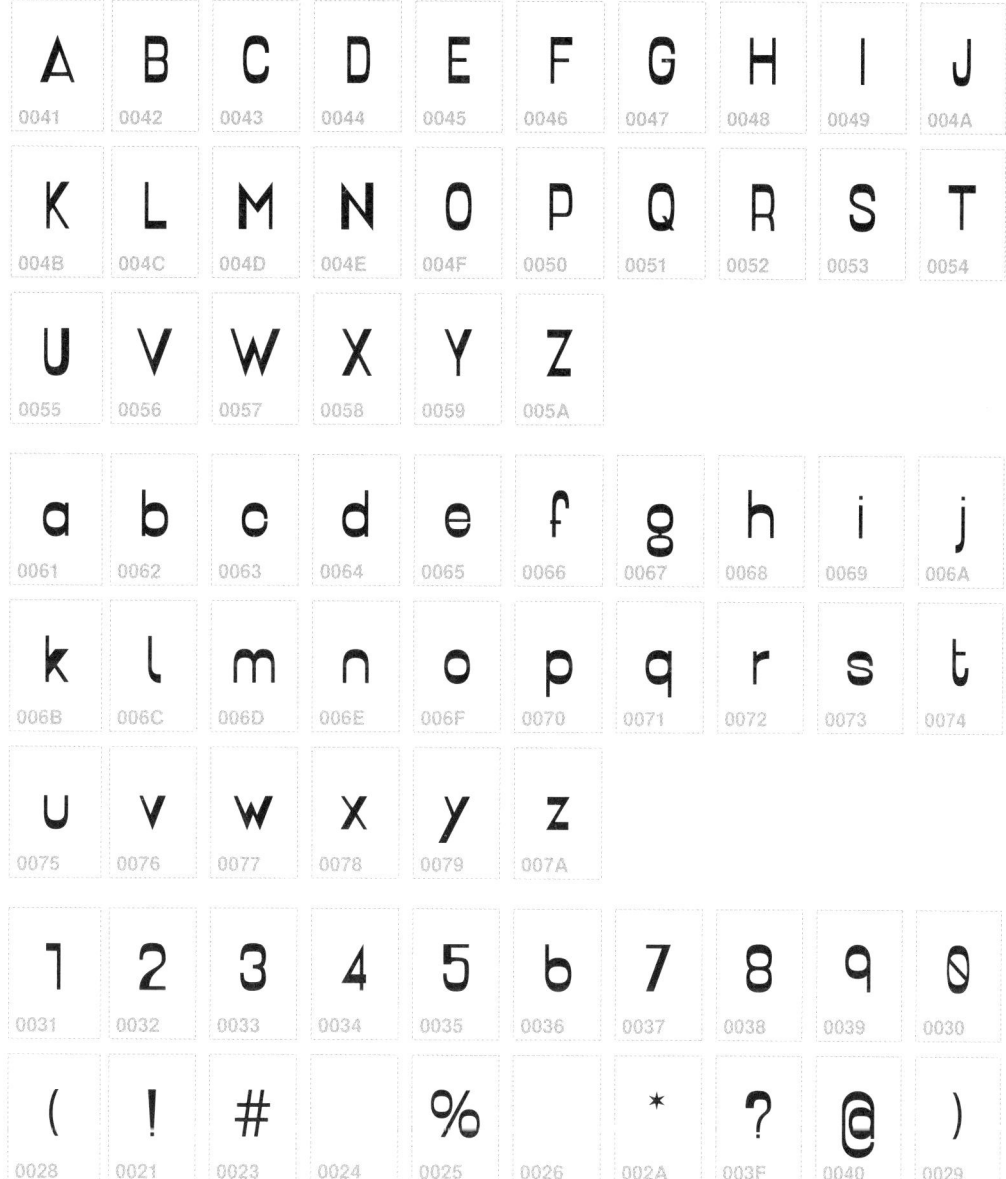

Moscou U.R.
Bilal Sebei

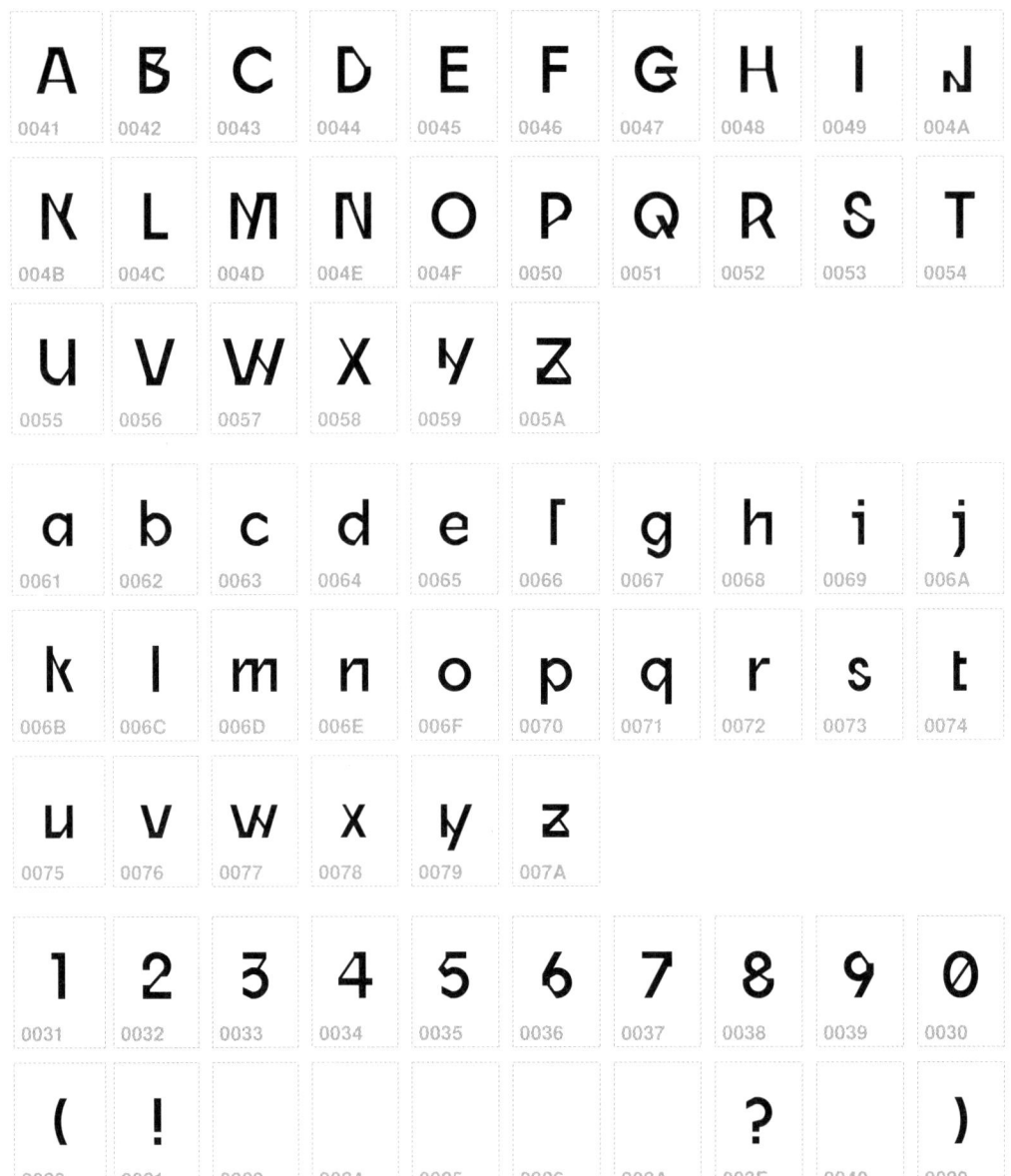

A 0041 B 0042 C 0043 D 0044 E 0045 F 0046 G 0047 H 0048 I 0049 J 004A

K 004B L 004C M 004D N 004E O 004F P 0050 Q 0051 R 0052 S 0053 T 0054

U 0055 V 0056 W 0057 X 0058 Y 0059 Z 005A

a 0061 b 0062 c 0063 d 0064 e 0065 f 0066 g 0067 h 0068 i 0069 j 006A

k 006B l 006C m 006D n 006E o 006F p 0070 q 0071 r 0072 s 0073 t 0074

u 0075 v 0076 w 0077 x 0078 y 0079 z 007A

1 0031 2 0032 3 0033 4 0034 5 0035 6 0036 7 0037 8 0038 9 0039 0 0030

(0028 ! 0021 0023 0024 0025 0026 002A ? 003F 0040) 0029

Mue
Fabian Fohrer

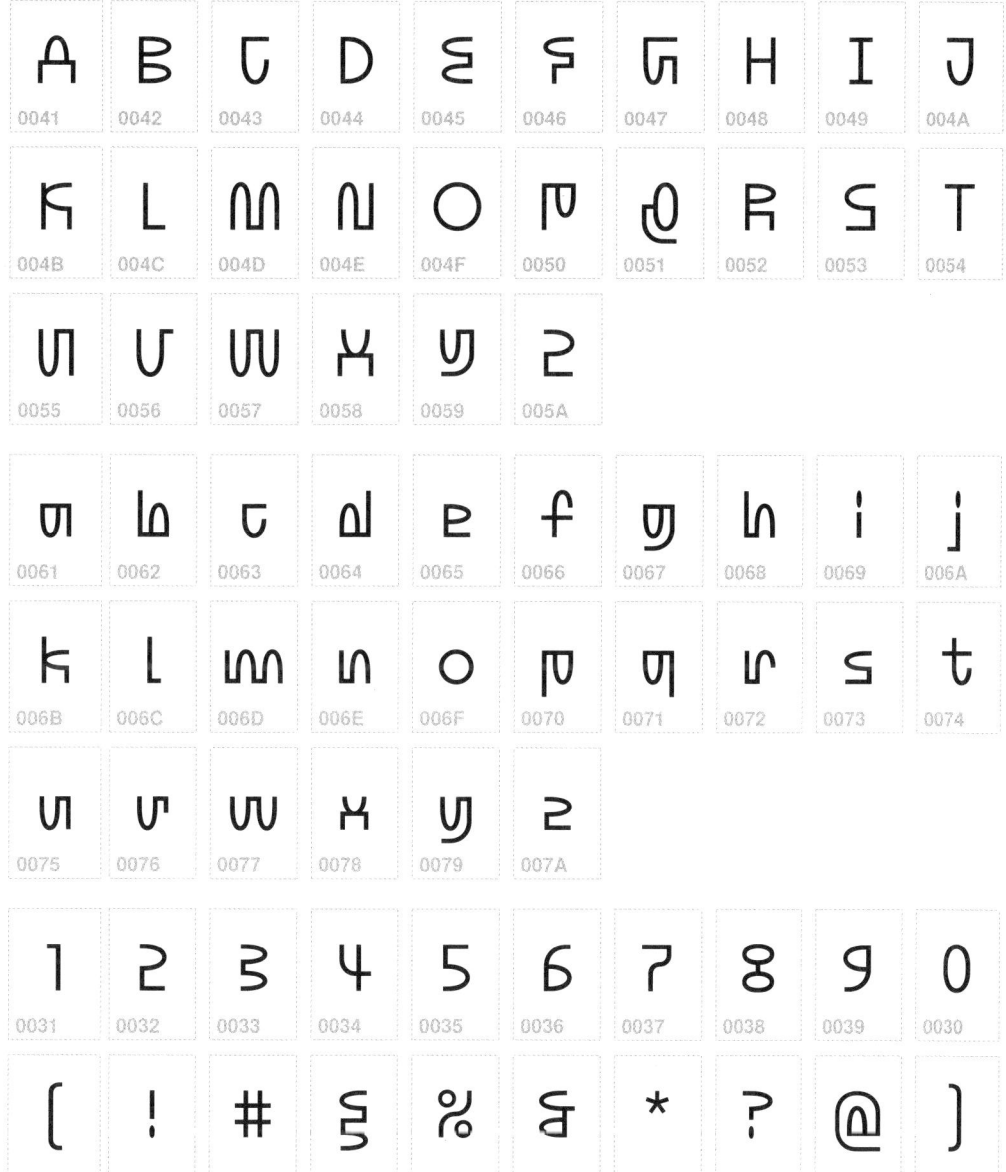

Mughal
Jose Houdini, Fabio Florez

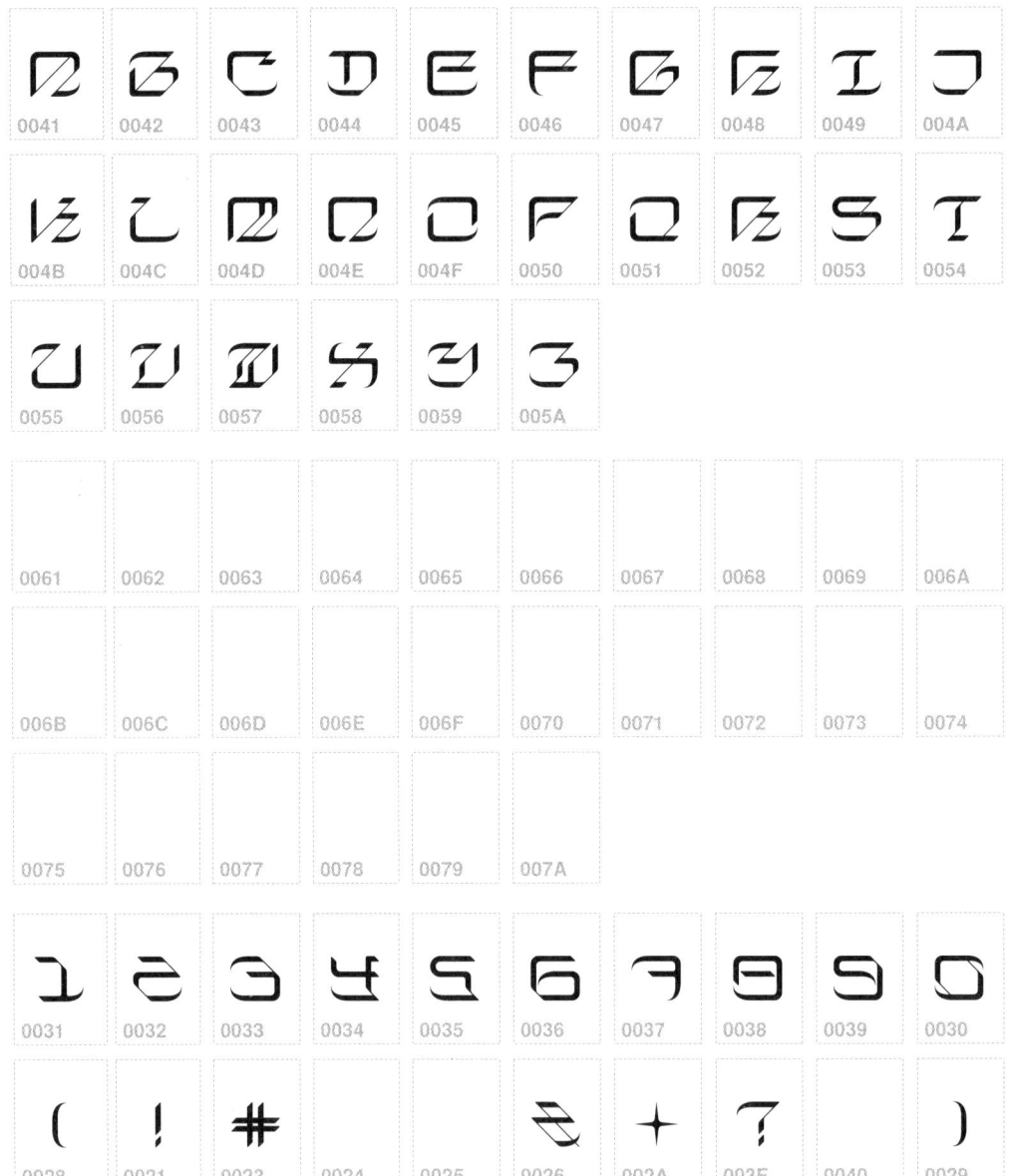

0041	0042	0043	0044	0045	0046	0047	0048	0049	004A
004B	004C	004D	004E	004F	0050	0051	0052	0053	0054
0055	0056	0057	0058	0059	005A				
0061	0062	0063	0064	0065	0066	0067	0068	0069	006A
006B	006C	006D	006E	006F	0070	0071	0072	0073	0074
0075	0076	0077	0078	0079	007A				
0031	0032	0033	0034	0035	0036	0037	0038	0039	0030
0028	0021	0023	0024	0025	0026	002A	003F	0040	0029

Mystica
Kevin Moll, Lena Manger

0041	0042	0043	0044	0045	0046	0047	0048	0049	004A
004B	004C	004D	004E	004F	0050	0051	0052	0053	0054
0055	0056	0057	0058	0059	005A				
0061	0062	0063	0064	0065	0066	0067	0068	0069	006A
006B	006C	006D	006E	006F	0070	0071	0072	0073	0074
0075	0076	0077	0078	0079	007A				
0031	0032	0033	0034	0035	0036	0037	0038	0039	0030
0028	0021	0023	0024	0025	0026	002A	003F	0040	0029

NAHEGLUT
Isabella Ramos Menzel

A	B	C	D	E	F	G	H	I	J
0041	0042	0043	0044	0045	0046	0047	0048	0049	004A
K	L	M	N	O	P	Q	R	S	T
004B	004C	004D	004E	004F	0050	0051	0052	0053	0054
U	V	W	X	Y	Z				
0055	0056	0057	0058	0059	005A				
a	b	c	d	e	f	g	h	i	j
0061	0062	0063	0064	0065	0066	0067	0068	0069	006A
k	l	m	n	o	p	q	r	s	t
006B	006C	006D	006E	006F	0070	0071	0072	0073	0074
u	v	w	x	y	z				
0075	0076	0077	0078	0079	007A				
0031	0032	0033	0034	0035	0036	0037	0038	0039	0030
	!								
0028	0021	0023	0024	0025	0026	002A	003F	0040	0029

Neustadt
Samara Keller

A	*B*	*C*	*D*	*E*	*F*	*G*	*H*	*I*	*J*
0041	0042	0043	0044	0045	0046	0047	0048	0049	004A
K	*L*	*M*	*N*	*O*	*P*	*Q*	*R*	*S*	*T*
004B	004C	004D	004E	004F	0050	0051	0052	0053	0054
U	*V*	*W*	*X*	*Y*	*Z*				
0055	0056	0057	0058	0059	005A				

0061	0062	0063	0064	0065	0066	0067	0068	0069	006A
006B	006C	006D	006E	006F	0070	0071	0072	0073	0074
0075	0076	0077	0078	0079	007A				

1	*2*	*3*	*4*	*5*	*6*	*7*	*8*	*9*	*0*
0031	0032	0033	0034	0035	0036	0037	0038	0039	0030
(	*!*	*#*			*&*		*?*	*@*	*)*
0028	0021	0023	0024	0025	0026	002A	003F	0040	0029

Noodle
Mălin Neamțu (Apriko Type Foundry)

ብ	฿	Ს	ꝺ	ꞡ	ꭵ	Ꮇ	Ꮃ	ꭴ	ꭴ
0041	0042	0043	0044	0045	0046	0047	0048	0049	004A
Ꮀ	Ꮄ	Ꮇ	Ꮇ	ꝋ	ꝓ	Ꮃ	Ꮄ	ꭶ	ꭲ
004B	004C	004D	004E	004F	0050	0051	0052	0053	0054
Ꮙ	Ꮙ	Ꮙ	ꞵ	ꭹ	ꭶ				
0055	0056	0057	0058	0059	005A				

0061	0062	0063	0064	0065	0066	0067	0068	0069	006A
006B	006C	006D	006E	006F	0070	0071	0072	0073	0074
0075	0076	0077	0078	0079	007A				

ꞁ	ꭶ	ꭶ	ꝯ	ꭶ	ꞇ	ꞔ	8	ꭷ	0
0031	0032	0033	0034	0035	0036	0037	0038	0039	0030
	!			%	℔	*	⁇	@	
0028	0021	0023	0024	0025	0026	002A	003F	0040	0029

Nostra
Lucas Descroix

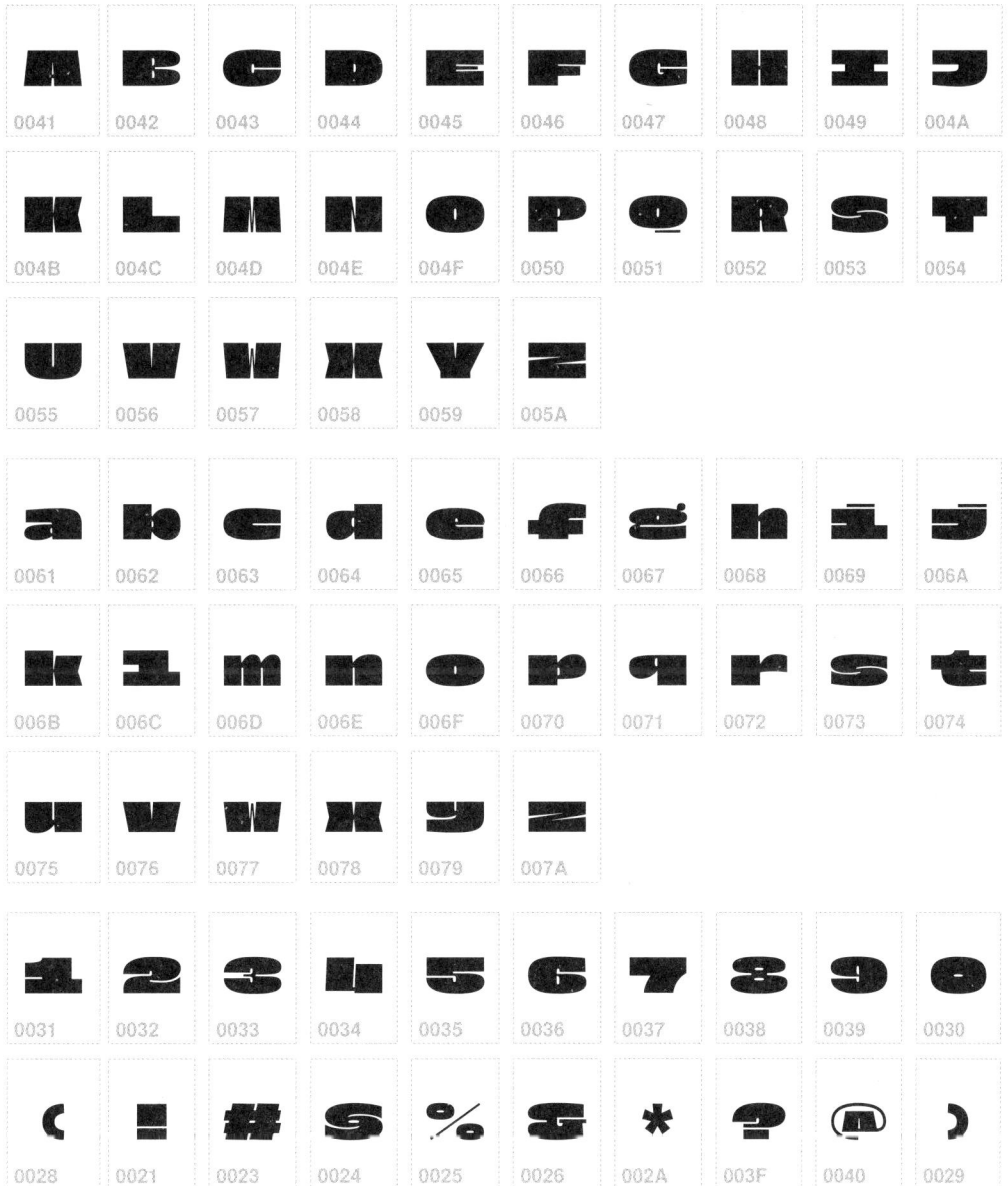

Nova
Kai Udema

ODB
Tobias Holzmann

Oskar
Robert Radziejewski

A	B	C	D	E	F	G	H	I	J
0041	0042	0043	0044	0045	0046	0047	0048	0049	004A
K	L	M	N	O	P	Q	R	S	T
004B	004C	004D	004E	004F	0050	0051	0052	0053	0054
U	V	W	X	Y	Z				
0055	0056	0057	0058	0059	005A				

A	B	C	D	E	F	G	H	I	J
0061	0062	0063	0064	0065	0066	0067	0068	0069	006A
K	L	M	N	O	P	Q	R	S	T
006B	006C	006D	006E	006F	0070	0071	0072	0073	0074
U	V	W	X	Y	Z				
0075	0076	0077	0078	0079	007A				

1	2	3	4	5	6	7	8	9	0
0031	0032	0033	0034	0035	0036	0037	0038	0039	0030
(	!						?	@	)
0028	0021	0023	0024	0025	0026	002A	003F	0040	0029

Pala
Stefano Bona

⊐	⊔	⊂	⊃	⊖	⊢	⊌	⊢	⊥	⌣
0041	0042	0043	0044	0045	0046	0047	0048	0049	004A
⊾	⌐	⊔	⊓	○	⊃	⊓	⊃	⊃	⊤
004B	004C	004D	004E	004F	0050	0051	0052	0053	0054
⊔	⊎	⊓	×	⊻	⊃				
0055	0056	0057	0058	0059	005A				

0061	0062	0063	0064	0065	0066	0067	0068	0069	006A
006B	006C	006D	006E	006F	0070	0071	0072	0073	0074
0075	0076	0077	0078	0079	007A				

⊿	⊏	⊐	⊔	⊆	⊏	⁊	⊗	⊖	○
0031	0032	0033	0034	0035	0036	0037	0038	0039	0030
0028	0021	0023	0024	0025	0026	002A	003F	0040	0029

Planet Caravan
Kirill Ratman

0041	0042	0043	0044	0045	0046	0047	0048	0049	004A
004B	004C	004D	004E	004F	0050	0051	0052	0053	0054
0055	0056	0057	0058	0059	005A				
0061	0062	0063	0064	0065	0066	0067	0068	0069	006A
006B	006C	006D	006E	006F	0070	0071	0072	0073	0074
0075	0076	0077	0078	0079	007A				
0031	0032	0033	0034	0035	0036	0037	0038	0039	0030
0028	0021	0023	0024	0025	0026	002A	003F	0040	0029

PLASTICWELT
Javier Rodriguez

0041	0042	0043	0044	0045	0046	0047	0048	0049	004A
004B	004C	004D	004E	004F	0050	0051	0052	0053	0054
0055	0056	0057	0058	0059	005A				
0061	0062	0063	0064	0065	0066	0067	0068	0069	006A
006B	006C	006D	006E	006F	0070	0071	0072	0073	0074
0075	0076	0077	0078	0079	007A				
0031	0032	0033	0034	0035	0036	0037	0038	0039	0030
0028	0021	0023	0024	0025	0026	002A	003F	0040	0029

Pluton
Benoît Canaud

Polyphem
Tobias Hönow

A	B	C	D	E	F	G	H	I	J
0041	0042	0043	0044	0045	0046	0047	0048	0049	004A
K	L	M	N	O	P	Q	R	S	T
004B	004C	004D	004E	004F	0050	0051	0052	0053	0054
U	V	W	X	Y	Z				
0055	0056	0057	0058	0059	005A				
a	b	c	d	e	f	g	h	i	j
0061	0062	0063	0064	0065	0066	0067	0068	0069	006A
k	l	m	n	o	p	q	r	s	t
006B	006C	006D	006E	006F	0070	0071	0072	0073	0074
u	v	w	x	y	z				
0075	0076	0077	0078	0079	007A				
1	2	3	4	5	6	7	8	9	0
0031	0032	0033	0034	0035	0036	0037	0038	0039	0030
(					&		?	@	)
0028	0021	0023	0024	0025	0026	002A	003F	0040	0029

Portico
Laura Hilbert

A	B	C	D	E	F	G	H	I	J
0041	0042	0043	0044	0045	0046	0047	0048	0049	004A
K	L	M	N	O	P	Q	R	S	T
004B	004C	004D	004E	004F	0050	0051	0052	0053	0054
U	V	W	X	Y	Z				
0055	0056	0057	0058	0059	005A				
a	b	c	d	e	f	g	h	i	j
0061	0062	0063	0064	0065	0066	0067	0068	0069	006A
k	l	m	n	o	p	q	r	s	t
006B	006C	006D	006E	006F	0070	0071	0072	0073	0074
u	v	w	x	y	z				
0075	0076	0077	0078	0079	007A				
0031	0032	0033	0034	0035	0036	0037	0038	0039	0030
0028	0021	0023	0024	0025	0026	002A	003F	0040	0029

Repro
Erkin Karamemet (Dinamo)

A	B	C	D	E	F	G	H	I	J
0041	0042	0043	0044	0045	0046	0047	0048	0049	004A
K	L	M	N	O	P	Q	R	S	T
004B	004C	004D	004E	004F	0050	0051	0052	0053	0054
U	V	W	X	Y	Z				
0055	0056	0057	0058	0059	005A				
a	b	c	d	e	f	g	h	i	j
0061	0062	0063	0064	0065	0066	0067	0068	0069	006A
k	l	m	n	o	p	q	r	s	t
006B	006C	006D	006E	006F	0070	0071	0072	0073	0074
u	v	w	x	y	z				
0075	0076	0077	0078	0079	007A				
1	2	3	4	5	6	7	8	9	0
0031	0032	0033	0034	0035	0036	0037	0038	0039	0030
(	!	#	§	%	&	*	?	@	)
0028	0021	0023	0024	0025	0026	002A	003F	0040	0029

Ribaasu
Tien-Min Liao

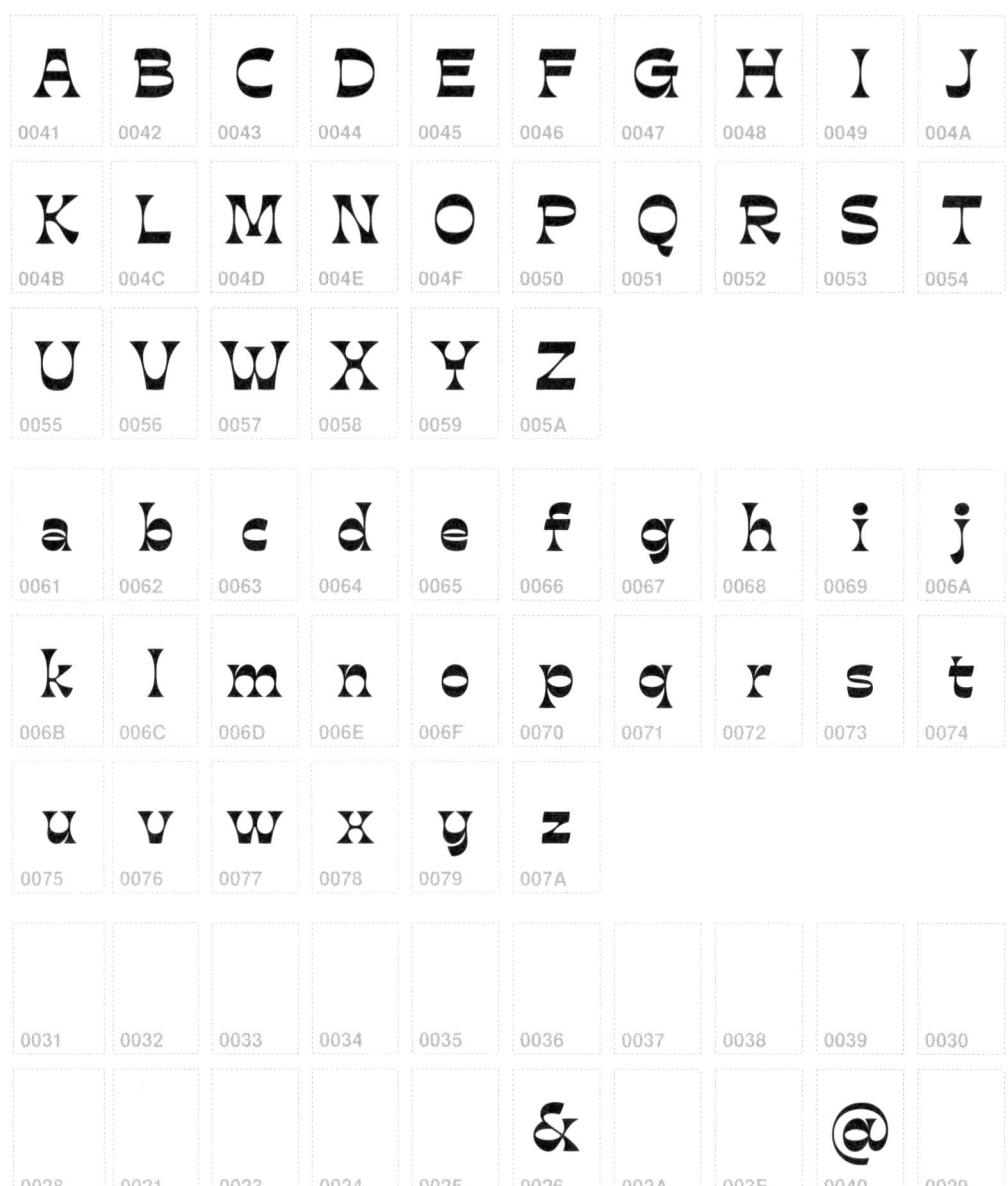

A	B	C	D	E	F	G	H	I	J
0041	0042	0043	0044	0045	0046	0047	0048	0049	004A
K	L	M	N	O	P	Q	R	S	T
004B	004C	004D	004E	004F	0050	0051	0052	0053	0054
U	V	W	X	Y	Z				
0055	0056	0057	0058	0059	005A				
a	b	c	d	e	f	g	h	i	j
0061	0062	0063	0064	0065	0066	0067	0068	0069	006A
k	l	m	n	o	p	q	r	s	t
006B	006C	006D	006E	006F	0070	0071	0072	0073	0074
u	v	w	x	y	z				
0075	0076	0077	0078	0079	007A				
0031	0032	0033	0034	0035	0036	0037	0038	0039	0030
					&			@	
0028	0021	0023	0024	0025	0026	002A	003F	0040	0029

Rygor
Maciej Połczyński

Serpe
Raphaël de La Morinerie

A	B	C	D	E	F	G	H	I	J
0041	0042	0043	0044	0045	0046	0047	0048	0049	004A
K	L	M	N	O	P	Q	R	S	T
004B	004C	004D	004E	004F	0050	0051	0052	0053	0054
U	V	W	X	Y	Z				
0055	0056	0057	0058	0059	005A				
a	b	c	d	e	f	g	h	i	j
0061	0062	0063	0064	0065	0066	0067	0068	0069	006A
k	l	m	n	o	p	q	r	s	t
006B	006C	006D	006E	006F	0070	0071	0072	0073	0074
u	v	w	x	y	z				
0075	0076	0077	0078	0079	007A				
0031	0032	0033	0034	0035	0036	0037	0038	0039	0030
0028	0021	0023	0024	0025	0026	002A	003F	0040	0029

Shrill
PizzaTypefaces

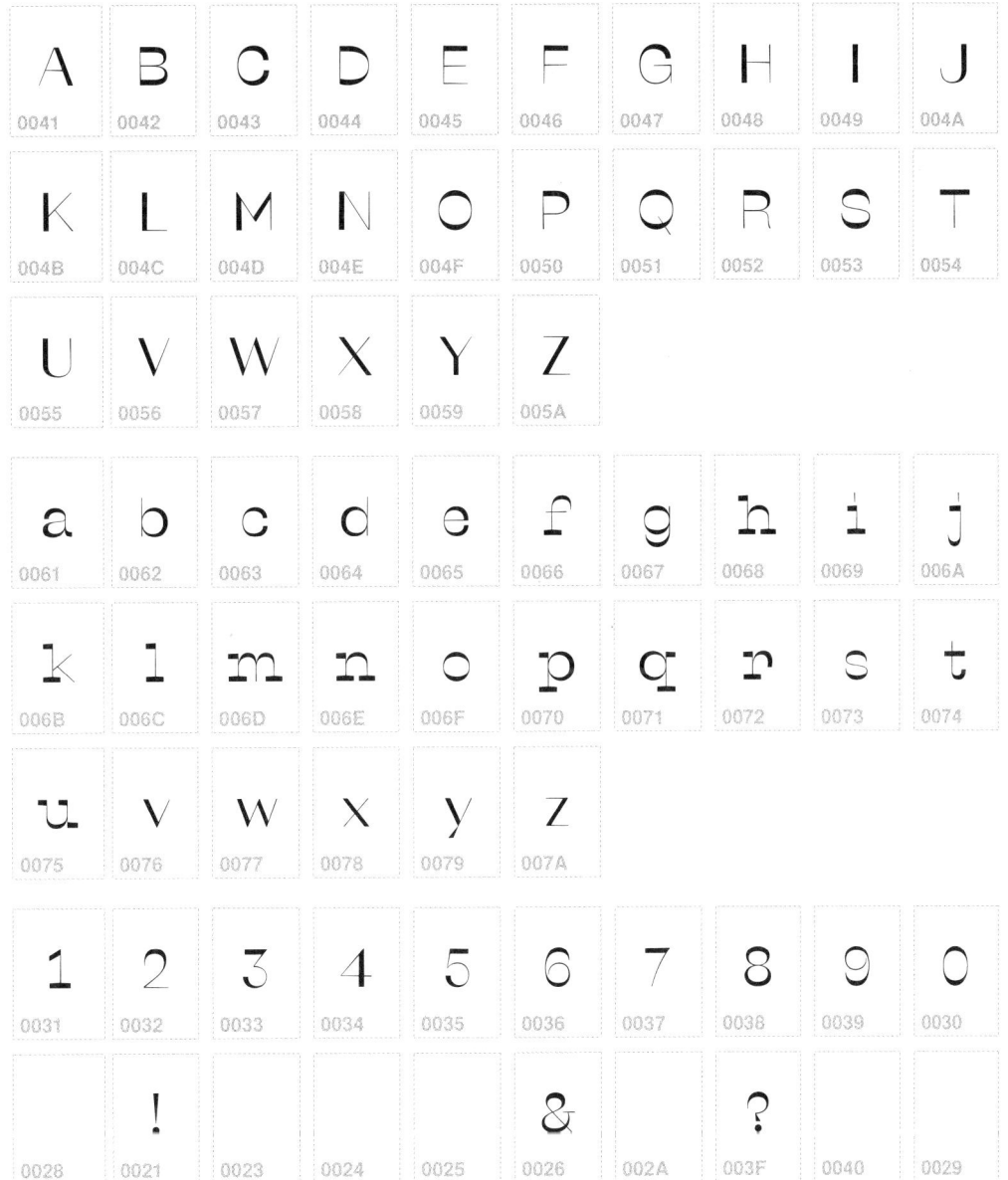

Siluett
Andree Paat (Tüpokompanii)

A	B	C	D	E	F	G	H	I	J
0041	0042	0043	0044	0045	0046	0047	0048	0049	004A
K	L	M	N	O	P	Q	R	S	T
004B	004C	004D	004E	004F	0050	0051	0052	0053	0054
U	V	W	X	Y	Z				
0055	0056	0057	0058	0059	005A				
a	b	c	d	e	f	g	h	i	j
0061	0062	0063	0064	0065	0066	0067	0068	0069	006A
k	l	m	n	o	p	q	r	s	t
006B	006C	006D	006E	006F	0070	0071	0072	0073	0074
u	v	w	x	y	z				
0075	0076	0077	0078	0079	007A				
1	2	3	4	5	6	7	8	9	0
0031	0032	0033	0034	0035	0036	0037	0038	0039	0030
(	!	#	§	%	&	*	?	@	)
0028	0021	0023	0024	0025	0026	002A	003F	0040	0029

Sketleton
Fabian Maier-Bode

A	B	C	D	E	F	G	H	I	J
0041	0042	0043	0044	0045	0046	0047	0048	0049	004A
K	L	M	N	O	P	Q	R	S	T
004B	004C	004D	004E	004F	0050	0051	0052	0053	0054
U	V	W	X	Y	Z				
0055	0056	0057	0058	0059	005A				
a	b	c	d	e	f	g	h	i	j
0061	0062	0063	0064	0065	0066	0067	0068	0069	006A
k	l	m	n	o	p	q	r	s	t
006B	006C	006D	006E	006F	0070	0071	0072	0073	0074
u	v	w	x	y	z				
0075	0076	0077	0078	0079	007A				
1	2	3	4	5	6	7	8	9	0
0031	0032	0033	0034	0035	0036	0037	0038	0039	0030
(	!	#	§		&	*	?	@	)
0028	0021	0023	0024	0025	0026	002A	003F	0040	0029

Solid
Alessio D'Ellena

Spirella
Jules Durand

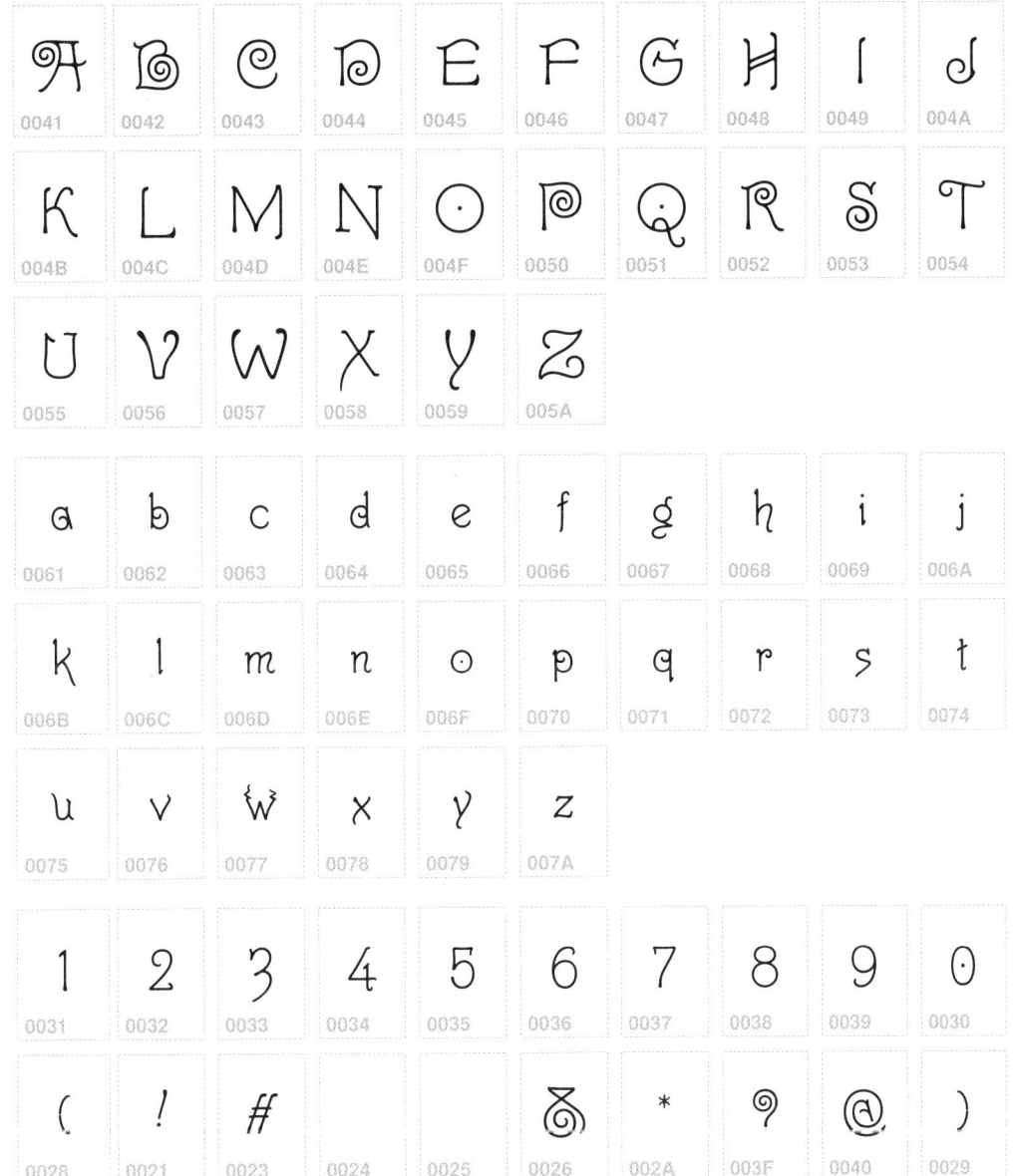

Streetfutura
Sascha Bente

A	B	C	D	E	F	G	H	I	J
0041	0042	0043	0044	0045	0046	0047	0048	0049	004A
K	L	M	N	O	P	Q	R	S	T
004B	004C	004D	004E	004F	0050	0051	0052	0053	0054
U	V	W	X	Y	Z				
0055	0056	0057	0058	0059	005A				

0061	0062	0063	0064	0065	0066	0067	0068	0069	006A
006B	006C	006D	006E	006F	0070	0071	0072	0073	0074
0075	0076	0077	0078	0079	007A				

1	2	3	4	5	6	7	8	9	0
0031	0032	0033	0034	0035	0036	0037	0038	0039	0030
(	!					*	?		)
0028	0021	0023	0024	0025	0026	002A	003F	0040	0029

Sveta

Aimur Takk (Tüpokompanii)

A	B	C	D	E	F	G	H	I	J
0041	0042	0043	0044	0045	0046	0047	0048	0049	004A
K	L	M	N	O	P	Q	R	S	T
004B	004C	004D	004E	004F	0050	0051	0052	0053	0054
U	V	W	X	Y	Z				
0055	0056	0057	0058	0059	005A				
a	b	c	d	e	f	g	h	i	j
0061	0062	0063	0064	0065	0066	0067	0068	0069	006A
k	l	m	n	o	p	q	r	s	t
006B	006C	006D	006E	006F	0070	0071	0072	0073	0074
u	v	w	x	y	z				
0075	0076	0077	0078	0079	007A				
1	2	3	4	5	6	7	8	9	0
0031	0032	0033	0034	0035	0036	0037	0038	0039	0030
(	!	#	§	%	&	*	?	@	)
0028	0021	0023	0024	0025	0026	002A	003F	0040	0029

SWORD
Kazuhiro Aihara

0041	0042	0043	0044	0045	0046	0047	0048	0049	004A
004B	004C	004D	004E	004F	0050	0051	0052	0053	0054
0055	0056	0057	0058	0059	005A				
0061	0062	0063	0064	0065	0066	0067	0068	0069	006A
006B	006C	006D	006E	006F	0070	0071	0072	0073	0074
0075	0076	0077	0078	0079	007A				
0031	0032	0033	0034	0035	0036	0037	0038	0039	0030
0028	0021	0023	0024	0025	0026	002A	003F	0040	0029

Taters
Tommi Sharp

A	B	C	D	E	F	G	H	I	J
0041	0042	0043	0044	0045	0046	0047	0048	0049	004A
K	L	M	N	O	P	Q	R	S	T
004B	004C	004D	004E	004F	0050	0051	0052	0053	0054
U	U	W	X	Y	Z				
0055	0056	0057	0058	0059	005A				
a	b	c	d	e	f	g	h	i	j
0061	0062	0063	0064	0065	0066	0067	0068	0069	006A
k	l	m	n	o	p	q	r	s	t
006B	006C	006D	006E	006F	0070	0071	0072	0073	0074
u	v	w	x	y	z				
0075	0076	0077	0078	0079	007A				
1	2	3	4	5	6	7	8	9	0
0031	0032	0033	0034	0035	0036	0037	0038	0039	0030
(	!	#	§	%	&	*	?	@	)
0028	0021	0023	0024	0025	0026	002A	003F	0040	0029

Urushi
Calvin Kwok

A	B	C	D	E	F	G	H	I	J
0041	0042	0043	0044	0045	0046	0047	0048	0049	004A
K	L	M	N	O	P	Q	R	S	T
004B	004C	004D	004E	004F	0050	0051	0052	0053	0054
U	V	W	X	Y	Z				
0055	0056	0057	0058	0059	005A				
a	b	c	d	e	f	g	h	i	j
0061	0062	0063	0064	0065	0066	0067	0068	0069	006A
k	l	m	n	o	p	q	r	s	t
006B	006C	006D	006E	006F	0070	0071	0072	0073	0074
u	v	w	x	y	z				
0075	0076	0077	0078	0079	007A				
1	2	3	4	5	6	7	8	9	0
0031	0032	0033	0034	0035	0036	0037	0038	0039	0030
(	!	#				*	?		)
0028	0021	0023	0024	0025	0026	002A	003F	0040	0029

VZWO Elephant
Viktor Zumegen

A	B	C	D	E	F	G	H	I	J
0041	0042	0043	0044	0045	0046	0047	0048	0049	004A
K	L	M	N	O	P	Q	R	S	T
004B	004C	004D	004E	004F	0050	0051	0052	0053	0054
U	V	W	X	Y	Z				
0055	0056	0057	0058	0059	005A				
a	b	c	d	e	f	g	h	i	j
0061	0062	0063	0064	0065	0066	0067	0068	0069	006A
k	l	m	n	o	p	q	r	s	t
006B	006C	006D	006E	006F	0070	0071	0072	0073	0074
u	v	w	x	y	z				
0075	0076	0077	0078	0079	007A				
1	2	3	4	5	6	7	8	9	0
0031	0032	0033	0034	0035	0036	0037	0038	0039	0030
(	!	#	$	%	&	*	?	@	)
0028	0021	0023	0024	0025	0026	002A	003F	0040	0029

Zangezi
Daria Cohen

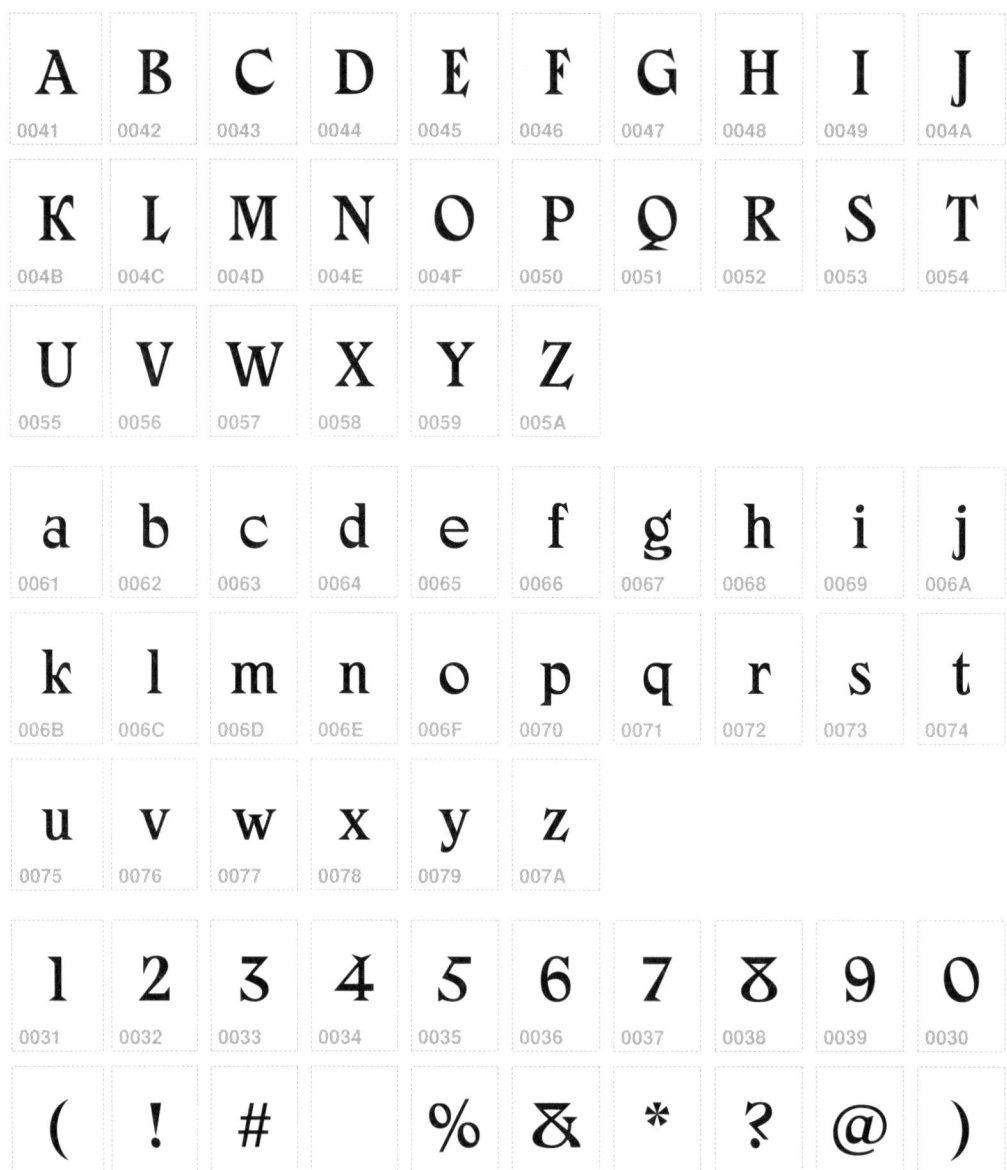

Zorn
Laura Csocsán

0041	0042	0043	0044	0045	0046	0047	0048	0049	004A
004B	004C	004D	004E	004F	0050	0051	0052	0053	0054
0055	0056	0057	0058	0059	005A				
a	b	c	d	e	f	g	h	i	j
0061	0062	0063	0064	0065	0066	0067	0068	0069	006A
k	l	m	n	o	p	q	r	s	t
006B	006C	006D	006E	006F	0070	0071	0072	0073	0074
u	v	w	x	y	z				
0075	0076	0077	0078	0079	007A				
1	2	3	4	5	6	7	8	9	0
0031	0032	0033	0034	0035	0036	0037	0038	0039	0030
(	!	#	$	%	&	*	?	@	)
0028	0021	0023	0024	0025	0026	002A	003F	0040	0029

New Aesthetic 1
A Collection of Experimental and Independent Type Design

Editors
Leonhard Laupichler
Sophia Brinkgerd

Publisher
Sorry Press
www.sorry-press.com

Content Direction
Lukas Kubina

Design Direction
Wiegand von Hartmann
Moritz Wiegand, Sophie von Hartmann,
Maya Bendel

Production
KOPA

Printed in Lithuania
ISBN 978-3-9102651-5-8

With thanks to Rüdiger Quass v. Deyen, Paul Bičište, Jakob Runge, Philipp Bulk